Rings That Bind

Cheryl Phillips

and

Linda Pysto

May the Rings That Bind be Ones of Love

God Bless

Thank you for your support and encouragement:
Gary Phillips, Tom Pysto, Nicholas Pysto, Mike Steele, Cindee Kopfman, Bertha Carnal, Frances Steele

Thank you for testing our patterns and proofreading:
Brooke Jeschke, Vicky Beckner, Diane Lippit, Laural Thompson, Barbara Gary, Cinda Farrell, Charlene Edwards, Kibbie Balsick, Jan Shuping, Judy Case, Sherilan Arterburn, Karla Shulz, Evelyn Lucht, and Pat Steele

Thank you for your contributions:
Donna Reppo, Parachute, Colorado
Nancy's Quilt Shop, Las Vegas, Nevada
Northcott Fabrics Inc.
Holly Holderman of LakeHouseDirect Fabrics
Hobbs Batting
Superior Threads

Acknowledgements:
All quilts shown in this book were made by Cheryl Phillips and/or Linda Pysto.
Printed by Colorado Printing Company, Grand Junction, Colorado
Photography by Dillard Jenkins of Colorado Photo Design, Grand Junction, Colorado
Plastic Templates by Phillips Fiber Art, Fruita, Colorado
Screen Printing by Brad Yenter, ATS Screen Printing, Grand Junction, Colorado

Contents

Meet the Authors

Cheryl Phillips

I am forever indebted to the wonderful friends I've met through quilting. They challenge me to find new ways to do things.

Growing up in a family that nurtured creativity was a blessing. Thanks to my mom who taught me to ask "what if?"

My husband, Gary, and I run Phillips Fiber Art from our home in Fruita, Colorado. Our adult daughters, Becky and Brooke, encourage our efforts, while our grandson, Hunter,is the cutest most adorable child ever born.

My best to you,

Cheryl

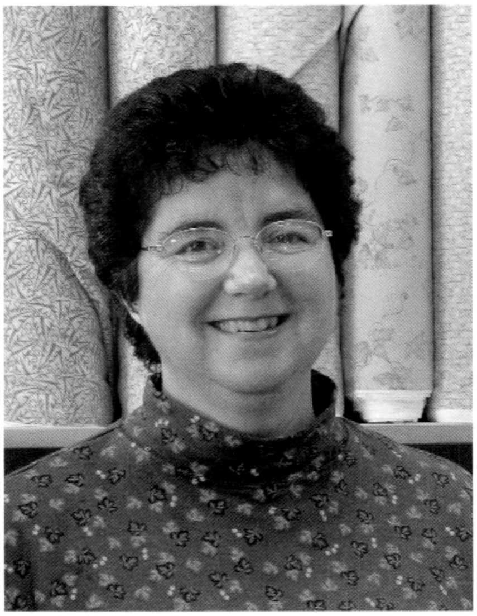

Linda Pysto

Quilting satisfies my hunger for a creative outlet like no other activity I do. After 20 plus years, I still find it satisfying and challenging. My favorite part of quilting is teaching beginners and watching them find the joy in it.

My husband, Tom, and I have lived in Las Vegas, Nevada for 16 years. We have two grown sons, Nicholas and Ben.

Many thanks to all my family, friends, and co-workers.

God bless, and may the rings that bind be ones of love.

Linda

A Few of Our Favorite Things

Nancy's Quilt Shop
Don't miss visiting her shop while traveling:
3290 N. Buffalo Dr., Suite 120
Las Vegas, NV 89129 phone: (702) 839-2779,
or visit her web site, www.nancysquiltshop.com She has awesome fabrics.

Hobbs Batting
It's the best batting around. You've got to try their new fusible cotton.

Light Bulb Moments
The moments of creativity on a road trip together
when ideas came faster than the miles went by.
The moment Nicholas bopped in with "the arc is too fat".
The moment Frances gave our book it's title, Rings That Bind.

To be honest, we love our new technique.
Block by block makes quilting fun again.

Overview of the Block by Block Process

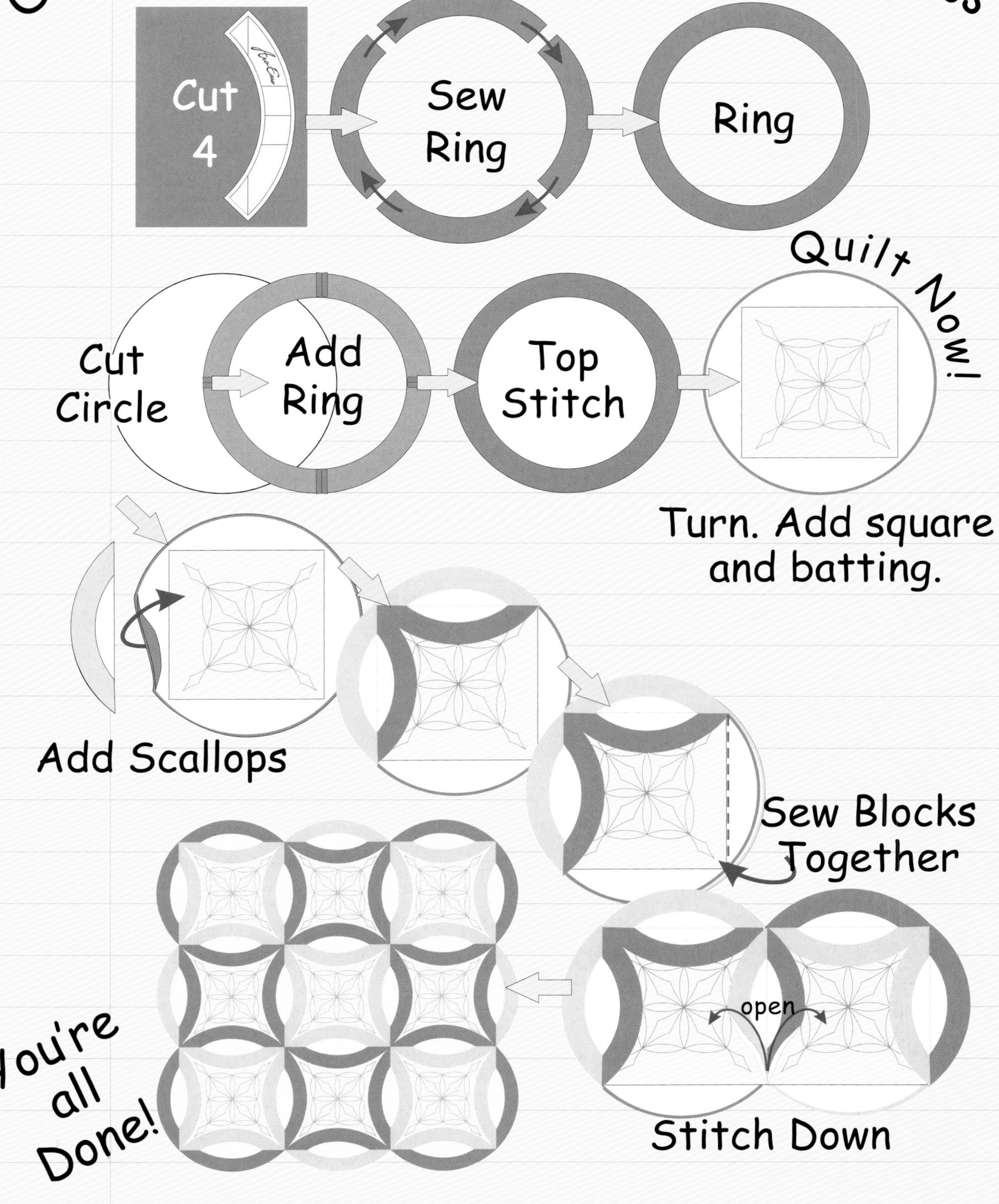
Cut
4
Sew
Ring
Ring
Quilt Now!
Cut
Circle
Add
Ring
Top
Stitch
Turn. Add square
and batting.
Add Scallops
Sew Blocks
Together
open
Stitch Down
You're
all
Done!

Fabric Selection

Be sure to read about fabrics before getting started.

Ring Fabric

Interlocking rings, like those exchanged by the bride and groom, give the Wedding Ring it's name. The *Rings That Bind* method uses four arcs sewn together to make each ring. Rings can be one, two, or a variety of colors. For a Double Wedding Ring, two color families are used to make the interlocking rings. You can vary the fabric combinations in many creative ways.
Create and color your own design using the grid found on page 53.

Pieced Arc Rings

You can achieve the illusion of many small pieces forming an arc without the tedious effort of sewing them together one by one. Strips of fabric are sewn together into strip sets, then arcs are cut from the strip sets. For rings to read as a unit, choose fabrics close in value and color. If one fabric dominates, the arc will be secondary to it. The *Rainbow* quilt uses an array of colors, but all are of a similar value and brightness. The "S" fabric choices will make up the block corners.

Seamless Arc Rings

Use a single piece of fabric for seamless arc wedding rings. The *China Blue* quilt uses two fabrics in the arcs. The *Imperial Wedding* quilt uses a variety of fabrics for each design element, yet the fabrics are united by both color and theme.

Interior Square Fabric

The interior square is the area on the front of the quilt in the center of the rings. When the same fabric is used for both the interior square and the football area, the interlocking rings will be the strongest design element. Choosing a contrasting or large scale fabric for the interior square will bring the focus to the center of the rings.
The interior square is an ideal showcase for skills such as ribbon embroidery or applique. It can be a canvas for your painting, stenciling or color crayon artwork. Display your thread sketching, quilting, trapunto, or designs from your embroidery machine. The smallest distance across the interior square is 7". To preview large prints use the stencil shown on page 54.

Backing Fabric

The backing fabric is also part of the front of your quilt, so it's selection is crucial to the success of your quilt. Backing fabric is cut into circles, then folded to the front to form half of the football area. Backing can be a single fabric or pieced from several different fabrics. Because the backing fabric is used on both front and back of your quilt, plus the scallop pieces, the required yardage may appear quite overwhelming. Test fabrics for shrinkage, particularly muslin or solid broadcloth. Prewashing is recommended to avoid uneven shrinkage during construction.

Batting Selection

For the block by block technique to be successful, use a flat batting. Save your fluffy polyester batting for another project. We have had excellent results with the new fusible cotton batting from Hobbs. Other choices include cotton battings such as Hobbs 80/20 Heirloom or 100% bleached cotton batting. Cotton flannel, prewashed several times, may also be substituted for batting.

Fabric Preparation

Test your fabric for shrinkage before cutting. If your backing fabric shrinks, your backing circles will be distorted. Pre-shrinking will eliminate the problem.

Notions

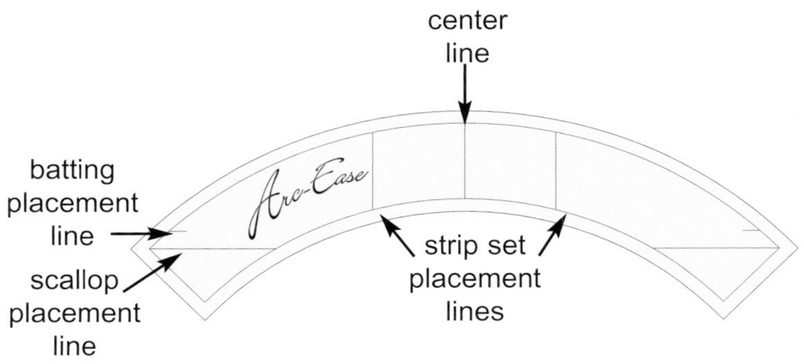
center line
batting placement line
scallop placement line
strip set placement lines
Arc-Ease

The Arc-Ease Tool

One tool with so many uses: cut circles, arcs, quarter circles, and scallops.

The Arc-Ease tool is precision cut acrylic and ideal for rotary cutting. Applying loops of wide transparent packaging tape, sticky side out, to the back of the tool keeps the template from slipping.

Try the tape.
It really works!

Rulers

A 12 1/2" square ruler is used to cut the block interior square, batting, and for marking the backing fabric. A standard 6" x 24" ruler is used for cutting strips.

Thread

Block by block ***construction*** requires quality cotton thread. For maximum strength set your machine for a short stitch length. Thread tension should be perfectly balanced.

Choices for ***quilting*** threads are numerous: cotton, rayon, metallic, or variegated, in blending or contrasting colors. The Bottom Line thread from Superior Threads is a good choice for bobbin thread when working with metallic or decorative threads.

Pins and Needles

Straight pins should be long and strong to accommodate the thicknesses. A fine milliners #10 needle works best for the hand sewing of the scallop arcs. A quilting (between) needle is suggested for cinching the block intersections.

Basting Tools

505™ Basting Glue Spray is helpful for basting the batting, backing and square together. Using the Hobbs Heirloom Fusible Batting eliminates the need for basting tools.

Marking Tools

There are many pencils and markers designed for marking on fabric. Most of the marking you will need to do is on the wrong side of the fabric. The line marked for the 12" stitching lines should be fine, definite, and not rub off easily. If your fabric is opaque, a lead pencil may be used. Fine chalk or white pencils may be used on dark fabrics. If marking doesn't work, you can baste, using a line of long machine stitching, to mark the guide line.

Yardage

Yardage figures are calculated to the nearest standard cut made at fabric stores, then one-eighth yard is added to allow for straightening. There is ***no extra*** yardage included for shrinkage or mistakes. Buy according to your own preferences, keeping these factors in mind.

One Color Rings

Seamless Arc Wedding Ring	Single 1	Runner 1 x 3	Wall 2 x 2	Baby 3 x 3	Lap 5 x 5	Twin 5 x 7	Double 6 x 7	Queen 7 x 8	King 8 x 8
Backing /Scallop Fabric	3/4 yd	1 3/4 yd	1 3/4 yd	3 3/8 yd	7 7/8 yd	10 3/4 yd	12 3/8 yd	16 1/4 yd	18 1/4 yd
Interior Squares	1/2 yd	1/2 yd	7/8 yd	1 1/4 yd	3 1/4 yd	4 1/2 yd	5 1/4 yd	6 7/8 yd	8 yd
One Color Arcs	1/2 yd	7/8 yd	7/8 yd	1 5/8 yd	3 3/4 yd	5 3/8 yd	6 1/2 yd	8 1/4 yd	9 yd

Two Color Rings

Seamless Arc Wedding Ring	Single 1	Runner 1 x 3	Wall 2 x 2	Baby 3 x 3	Lap 5 x 5	Twin 5 x 7	Double 6 x 7	Queen 7 x 8	King 8 x 8
Backing /Scallop Fabric	3/4 yd	1 3/4 yd	1 3/4 yd	3 3/8 yd	7 7/8 yd	10 3/4 yd	12 3/8 yd	16 3/8 yd	18 3/8 yd
Interior Squares	1/2 yd	1/2 yd	7/8 yd	1 1/4 yd	3 1/4 yd	4 5/8 yd	5 1/4 yd	6 7/8 yd	8 yd
Two Color Arcs	1/2 yd each	1/2 yd each	1/2 yd each	7/8 yd each	2 yd each	3 yd each	3 1/2 yd each	4 1/4 yd each	4 5/8 yd each

Two Color Family Rings

Pieced Arc Wedding Ring	Single 1	Runner 1 x 3	Wall 2 x 2	Baby 3 x 3	Lap 5 x 5	Twin 5 x 7	Double 6 x 7	Queen 7 x 8	King 8 x 8
Backing /Scallop Fabric	3/4 yd	1 3/4 yd	1 3/4 yd	3 3/8 yd	7 7/8 yd	10 3/4 yd	12 3/8 yd	16 1/4 yd	18 3/8 yd
Interior Squares	1/2 yd	1/2 yd	7/8 yd	1 1/4 yd	3 1/4 yd	4 1/2 yd	5 1/4 yd	6 7/8 yd	8 yd
C and **D** Set 1 Strips **C** and **D** Set 2 Strips	1/4 yd each	1/4 yd each	1/4 yd each	3/8 yd each	1/2 yd each	3/4yd each	7/8 yd each	1 1/8 yd each	2 yd each
A, B, E, F Set 1 Strips **A, B, E, F** Set 2 Strips	1/4 yd each	1/4 yd each	1/4 yd each	1/4 yd each	3/8 yd each	5/8 yd each	3/4 yd each	7/8 yd each	7/8 yd each
S Set 1 Strips **S** Set 2 Strips	1/4 yd each	1/4 yd each	1/4 yd each	3/8 yd each	3/4 yd each	1 1/4 yd each	1 3/8 yd each	1 5/8 yd each	1 3/4 yd each

Batting	Single 1	Runner 1 x 3	Wall 2 x 2	Baby 3 x 3	Lap 5 x 5	Twin 5 x 7	Double 6 x 7	Queen 7 x 8	King 8 x 8
Bagged Cotton Batting	crib	crib	crib	crib	queen	queen	queen	queen	queen
Batting on a 90" roll	3/8 yd	3/8 yd	3/8 yd	3/4 yd	1 1/2 yd	2 1/4 yd	3 yd	3 3/8 yd	3 1/2 yd
Batting on a 45" roll	3/8 yd	3/4 yd	3/4 yd	1 3/8 yd	3 3/8 yd	4 3/8 yd	5 yd	5 1/2 yd	7 3/8 yd

Choosing your quilt size

We suggest you begin with a small project such as a single block or table runner.

Once you're familiar with the technique, select the size and variation you want to make. A word of warning: quilts larger than double size can be quite cumbersome in the final assembly stage. Rather than machine top stitching, you may want to hand stitch your flaps to the squares in the final step.

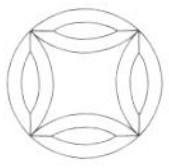

single
17" x 17"

runner
17" x 41"

wall
29" x 29"

baby
41" x 41"

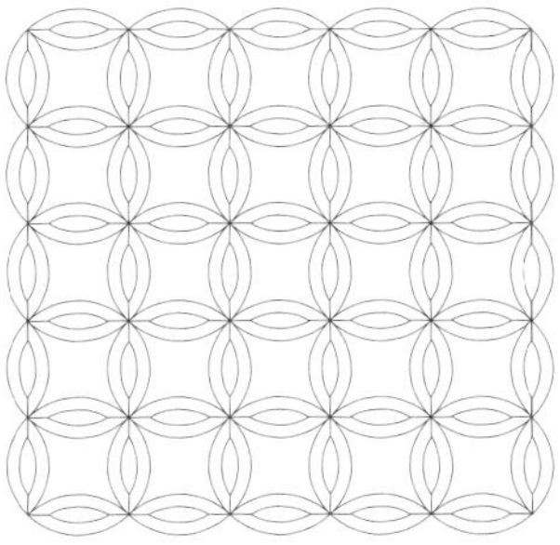

lap 64" x 64"

twin
64" x 90"

double
76" x 90"

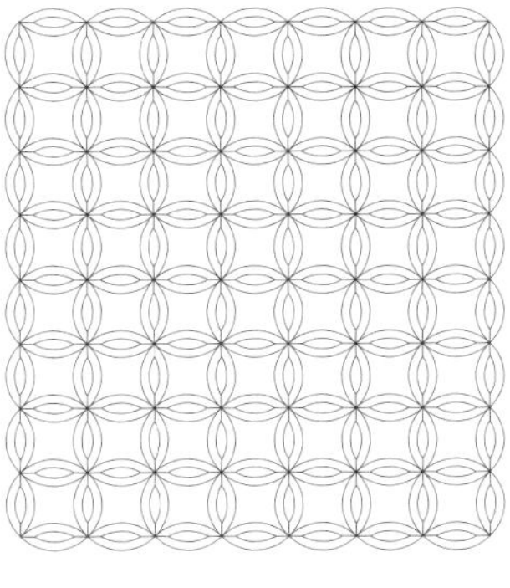

queen
90" x 100"

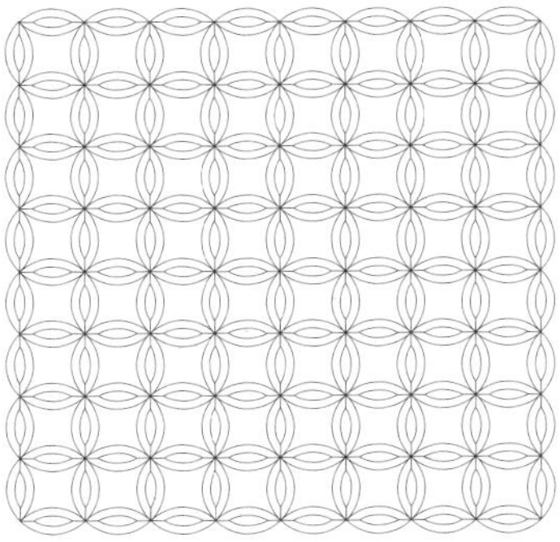

king
100" x 100"

Glossary

arc a fabric unit used to make rings

backing circle a circle making up the back of the quilt which also folds to the front to form half of the football areas in each block

block a unit made up of an interior square, arcs, batting, and backing

crease a pressed fold used for a marking or for placement purposes

flap when circles are sewn together the curved portion is referred to as a flap

football the shape of the area between the interlocking rings

front side-back side refers to the front and back of the quilt

guide line the square drawn on the wrong side of the backing circle, blocks are stitched together along this line

interior square a 12 1/2" square creating the center of the front of the block

right side-wrong side refers to the right and wrong side of the fabric

ring four fabric arcs sewn together to make a *ring*, then sewn to the backing circle

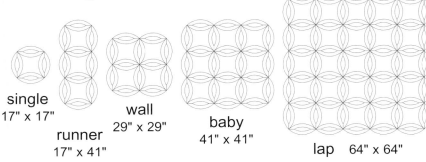

scallop makes the outside curved edge of the wedding ring quilt, when the scallop backing piece is open it is a football shape

Cutting Backing

Backing Circles

18" Squares	Single 1	Runner 1 x 3	Wall 2 x 2	Baby 3 x 3	Lap 5 x 5	Twin 5 x 7	Double 6 x 7	Queen 7 x 8	King 8 x 8
Backing Circles	1	3	4	9	25	35	42	56	64

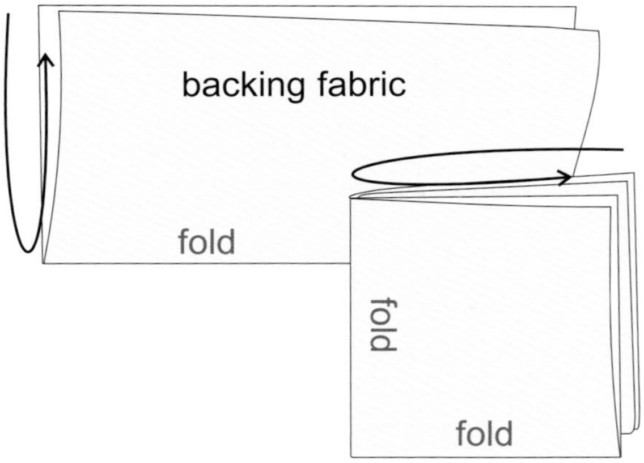
backing fabric
fold
fold
fold

Time Saving Tip

Reduce the bulk of a large piece of fabric by first tearing it into squares. Don't worry about the torn edges as you'll be cutting them off in the next step.

- First, clip the selvage and tear to establish the grain.
- Measure 18" along the selvage and clip a notch. Tear the piece crosswise.
- Notch the strip in 18" increments, tear two squares, and iron.
- Repeat for the number of background circles needed.

Cutting the Backing

- Cut 18" squares as listed above for your quilt size.
- Test your fabric square for shrinkage. See page 6 for more fabric concerns.

Fold the square into quarters:

- Fold in half.
- Press the fold.
- Fold in half again.
- Press the new fold.

Mark the 8 3/4" measurements on the square ruler with tape or a wipe off marker to make them easier to find.

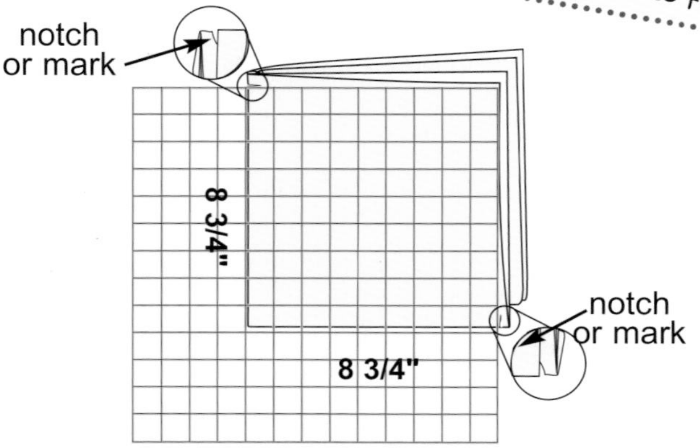
notch
or mark
8 3/4"
8 3/4"
notch
or mark

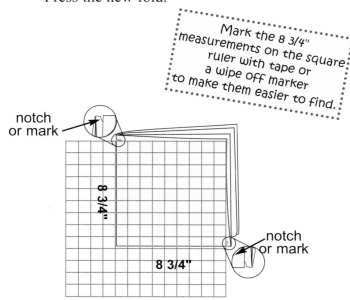

- Place a square ruler on the folded backing, aligning both 8 3/4" marks with the folded sides.
- Cut little notches, or mark to establish these points.

Cutting the Backing into Circles

- Place the Arc-Ease tool onto the folded fabric, aligning marked edge of the tool ***precisely*** with both 8 3/4" notches.
- Cut the square along the outer edge of the Arc-Ease tool into a circle.
- Measure the circle to be sure it's truly round and the diameter is exactly 17 1/2".

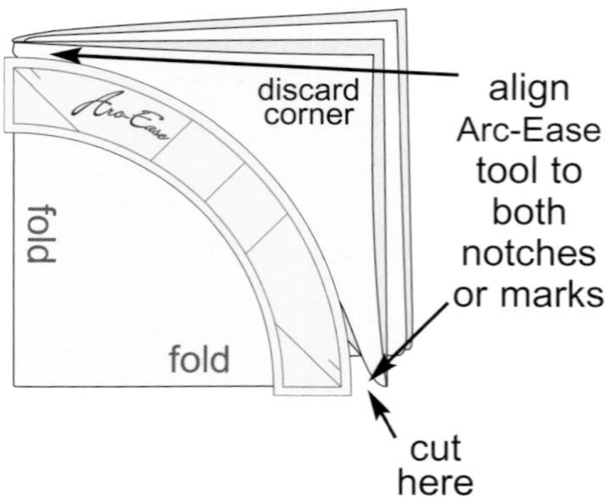
discard
corner
fold
fold
align
Arc-Ease
tool to
both
notches
or marks
cut
here

Cutting Seamless Wedding Ring Pieces

Interior Squares

Interior Squares	Single 1	Runner 1 x 3	Wall 2 x 2	Baby 3 x 3	Lap 5 x 5	Twin 5 x 7	Double 6 x 7	Queen 7 x 8	King 8 x 8
12 1/2" Squares	1	3	4	9	25	35	42	56	64

Cutting the Interior Squares

- Cut squares of interior fabric, referring to the chart above.
- Complete any applique or embroidery intended for the interior square before layering.
  - The applique pattern used for the front cover can be found on page 55.
  - Creative options for your interior squares can be found on page 46.

interior
square

Scallops

Scallops cut from 6 x 13" Strips of backing fabric	Single 1	Runner 1 x 3	Wall 2 x 2	Baby 3 x 3	Lap 5 x 5	Twin 5 x 7	Double 6 x 7	Queen 7 x 8	King 8 x 8
Total Number of Scallops	4	8	8	12	20	24	26	30	32

Cutting the Scallops

- Fold the 6" x 13" strip of backing fabric in half lengthwise with wrong sides together and press the fold.
- Place the Arc-Ease tool on the fabric, so that the horizontal lines are directly on the fold.
- Cut ***only*** along the outside edge of the Arc-Ease tool.
- Cut the number of scallops as listed in the chart above.

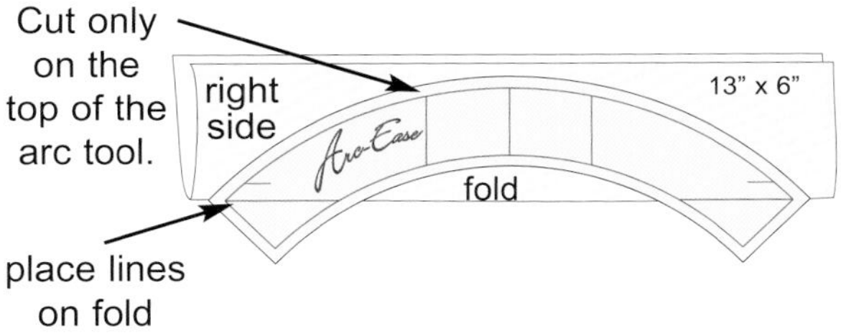
Cut only on the top of the arc tool.
right side
13" x 6"
Arc-Ease
fold
place lines on fold

Batting

Batting	Single 1	Runner 1 x 3	Wall 2 x 2	Baby 3 x 3	Lap 5 x 5	Twin 5 x 7	Double 6 x 7	Queen 7 x 8	King 8 x 8
11 1/2" Squares	1	3	4	9	25	35	42	56	64
Scallops	4	8	8	12	20	24	26	30	32

Cutting the Batting

- Referring to the chart, cut the 11 1/2" squares.
- To cut scallops of batting, place the Arc-Ease tool on batting with a straight edge of the batting lining up with the short lines on the arc tool.
- Cut ***only*** along the outside edge of the Arc-Ease tool.
- Trim the corners of the batting scallops.
- Set aside the scallop pieces for later use.

batting
for block

Cut 11 1/2" squares.

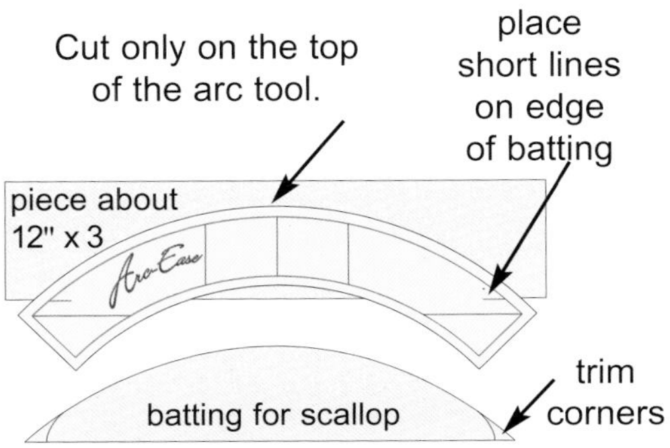
Cut only on the top of the arc tool.
place short lines on edge of batting
piece about 12" x 3
Arc-Ease
batting for scallop
trim corners

note: this is one layer and not folded.

Cutting Seamless Arcs

Strips

Strips cut across fabric width	Single 1	Runner 1 x 3	Wall 2 x 2	Baby 3 x 3	Lap 5 x 5	Twin 5 x 7	Double 6 x 7	Queen 7 x 8	King 8 x 8
One Color 13" wide strips	1	2	2	4	10	14	17	22	24
Fabric A and Fabric B 13" wide strips	1 each	1 each	1 each	2 each	5 each	7 each	9 each	11 each	12 each

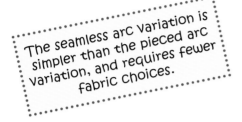

The seamless arc variation is simpler than the pieced arc variation, and requires fewer fabric choices.

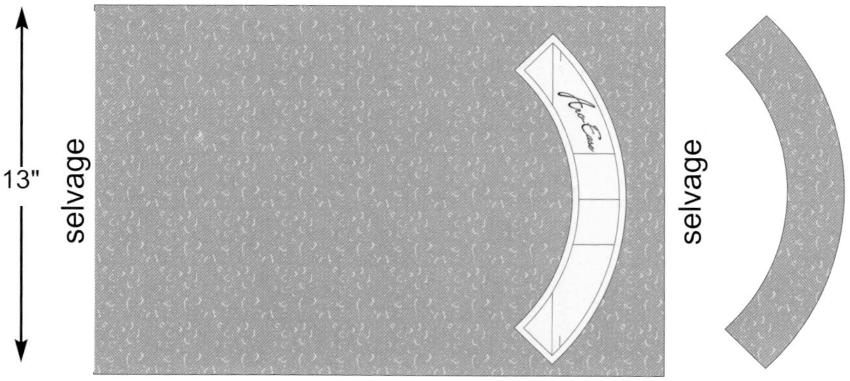

13"
selvage
selvage

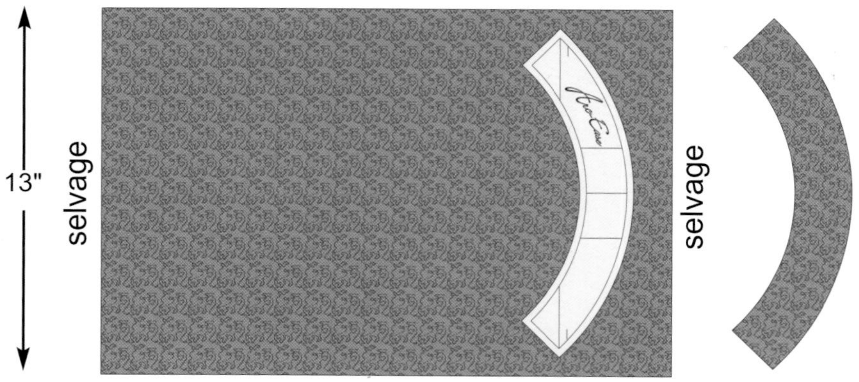

13"
selvage
selvage

Cutting Seamless Arcs

- Cut 13" wide strips of Fabric A and Fabric B as listed in the chart above.
- Prepare your Arc-Ease tool by applying loops of wide transparent packaging tape, sticky side out, to the back side of the tool. This will keep the Arc-Ease tool from slipping, assuring an accurate cut.
- Place the Arc-Ease tool onto the arc fabric as shown.
- Cut the number of arcs as listed in the chart below.
- Set aside arcs for later use with scallops as listed in the chart below.

One Color Arcs

Seamless Arcs	Single 1	Runner 1 x 3	Wall 2 x 2	Baby 3 x 3	Lap 5 x 5	Twin 5 x 7	Double 6 x 7	Queen 7 x 8	King 8 x 8
Total One Color Arcs	8	20	24	48	120	164	194	254	288
One Color Arcs set aside for scallops	4	8	8	12	20	24	26	30	32

Two Color Arcs

Fabric A and Fabric B Arcs	4 each	10 each	12 each	24 each	60 each	82 each	97 each	127 each	144 each
Fabric A Arcs set aside for scallops	0	2	4	4	8	10	13	15	16
Fabric B Arcs set aside for scallops	4	6	4	8	12	14	13	15	16

Seamless Rings

Making Rings

- Place two Fabric A arcs together, right sides facing.
- Sew the arcs together to make a pair. Sew with ***exact*** 1/4" seams.
- Sew two arc pairs together to make a ring of Fabric A.
- Press open the seams joining the arcs.
- Spray the arc with spray sizing. While wet, precisely fold under 1/4" along the inner curved edge.
- Press the fold being careful not to stretch the edge.
- Press the turned edge from the wrong side.
- Refer to the chart below and make the number of rings listed for the quilt size you've selected.
- Repeat for rings of Fabric B.

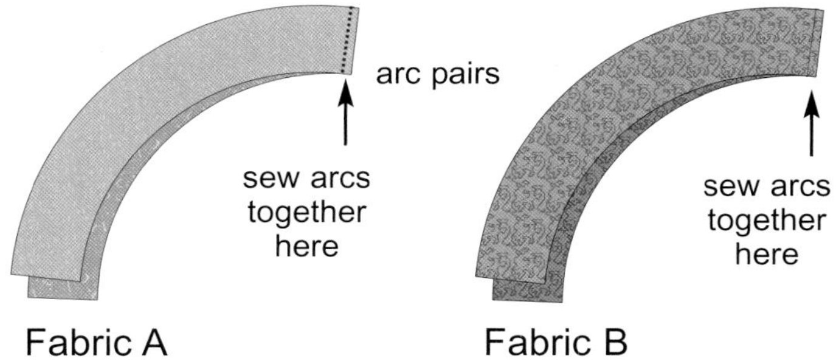
arc pairs
sew arcs together here
sew arcs together here
Fabric A
Fabric B

Here's a trick to make the folded edge smooth and even: stitch a scant 1/4" (less than) from the inner edge before folding to use as a pressing guide. This is similar to stay stitching used in clothing construction.

Hint: Spray sizing will help hold the folded edge in place.

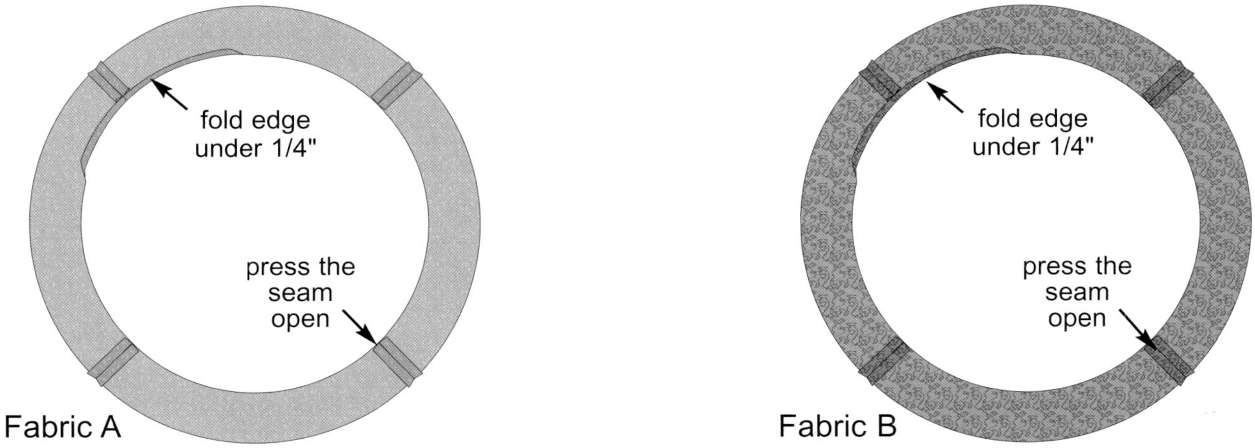
fold edge under 1/4"
press the seam open
Fabric A
fold edge under 1/4"
press the seam open
Fabric B

	Seamless Arc Version	Single 1	Runner 1 x 3	Wall 2 x 2	Baby 3 x 3	Lap 5 x 5	Twin 5 x 7	Double 6 x 7	Queen 7 x 8	King 8 x 8
One Color Rings	One Color Rings	1	3	4	9	25	35	42	56	64
Two Color Rings	Fabric A Rings	1	2	2	5	13	18	21	28	32
	Fabric B Rings	0	1	2	4	12	17	21	28	32

Backing Circles

- Open and refold the circle diagonally to establish precise eighth sections.
- Press the folds into creases. The creases will be used later for placement.

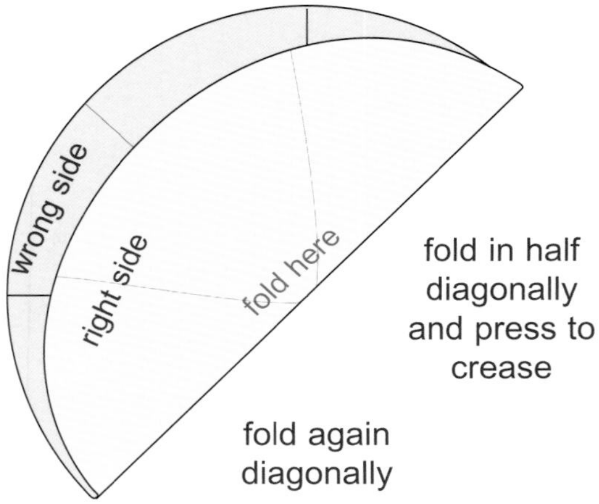
wrong side
right side
fold here
fold in half diagonally and press to crease
fold again diagonally

Marking the square on the backing circle is made simple, yet precise with our quilting stencils.
See page 56.

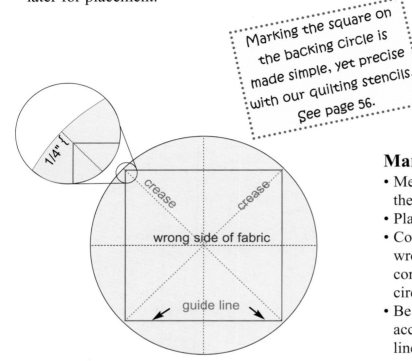

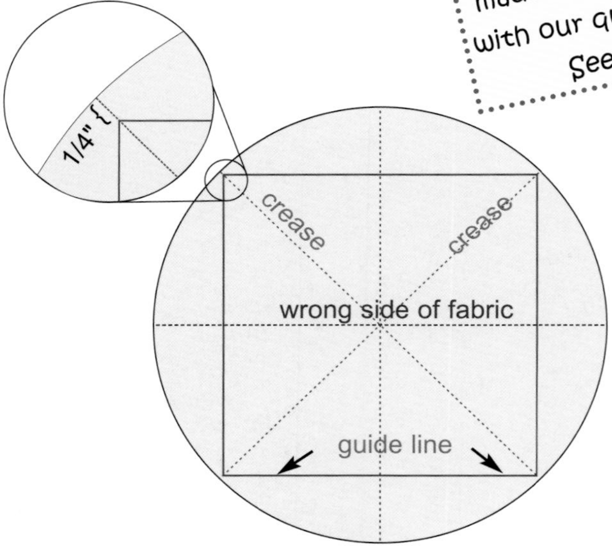
1/4"
crease
crease
wrong side of fabric
guide line

Marking the Backing Circle

- Measure along the diagonal crease 1/4" from the edge.
- Place a small dot at this point.
- Connecting the dots, draw a 12" square on the wrong side of the backing circle, with the corners of the square 1/4" from the edge of the circle and along the diagonal crease.
- Be sure you mark the lines of the square accurately. You'll be stitching along these guide lines when you sew the blocks together.

Sewing Rings to the Backing Circles

- Place the ***right*** side of the ring onto the ***wrong*** side of the backing circle.
- Match the arc seam to the diagonal crease line.
- Pin the ring to the circle, with raw edges even.
- Sew the ring to the circle, stitching ***exactly*** 1/4" from the outer edge. The stitching through the arc seam should intersect precisely with the corner of the marked square.

Are you using striped fabric for your arcs? Stripes require some special attention.
See page 50.

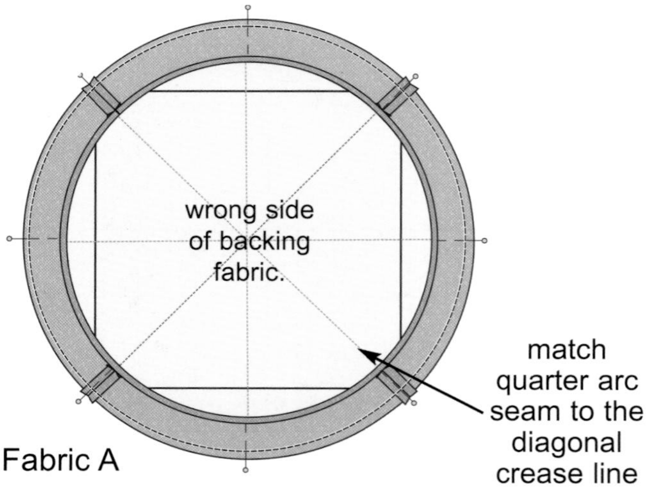
wrong side of backing fabric.
match quarter arc seam to the diagonal crease line
Fabric A

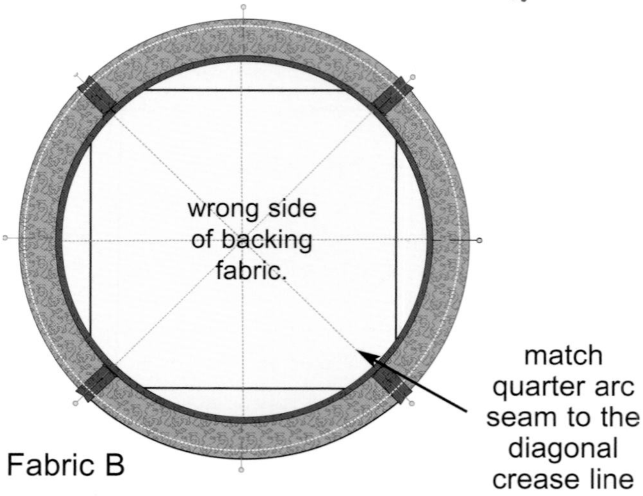
wrong side of backing fabric.
match quarter arc seam to the diagonal crease line
Fabric B

Top Stitching Seamless Rings

Turning the Ring

- Grade the seam.
- Holding your scissors nearly flat, trim the seam allowance slightly.

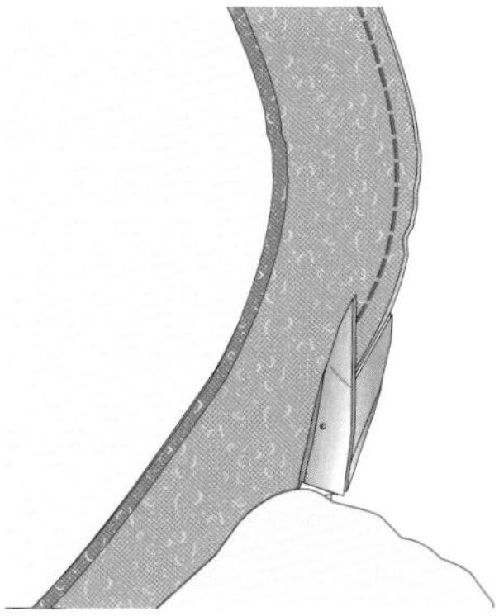

- Here are two suggestions to give a smooth edge and help eliminate any tucks along the curved edge.
  - Finger press the arc seam, smoothing the seam allowances toward the circle and away from the arc.
  - Stitch close to the circle seam on the side of the backing circle. The stitching goes through both seam allowances, in a similar manner to ***under stitching*** used in clothing construction.

Think of the ring as a facing.

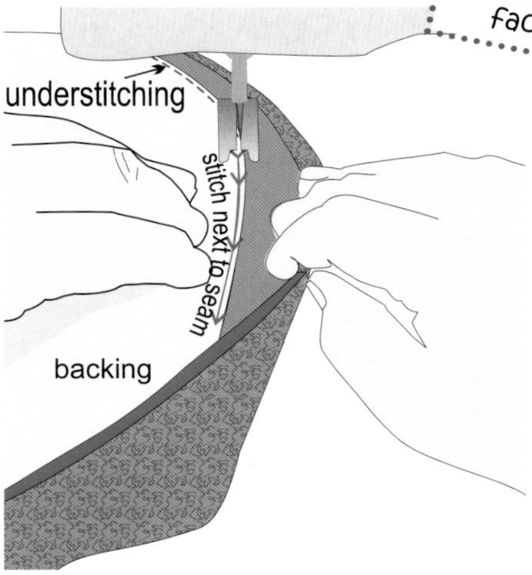
understitching
stitch next to seam
backing

- Bring the ring around the backing circle.
- When aligned, pin the ring in place at each crease line, matching seams to creases, keeping the folded edge of the ring parallel to the outer edge of the circle.
- Press the ring in place.

Top Stitching the Rings

- Top stitch very close to the folded inner edge.
- The top stitching is also called edge stitching. Sew approximately 1/16" from the folded edge. It is often helpful to lengthen the stitch for a smooth stitching line.
- Alternatives to top stitching include blind stitching with monofilament (clear) thread, decorative stitching with contrasting thread, or adding trim to cover the top stitching.

Before stitching down the ring: Examine your circle ring: Is the arc the same width all the way around?

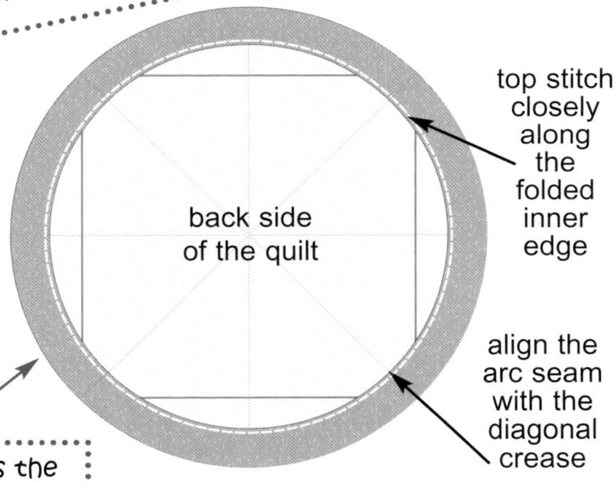
back side
of the quilt
top stitch closely along the folded inner edge
align the arc seam with the diagonal crease

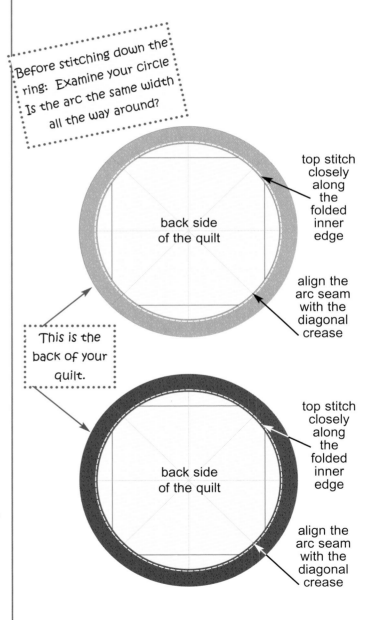

This is the back of your quilt.

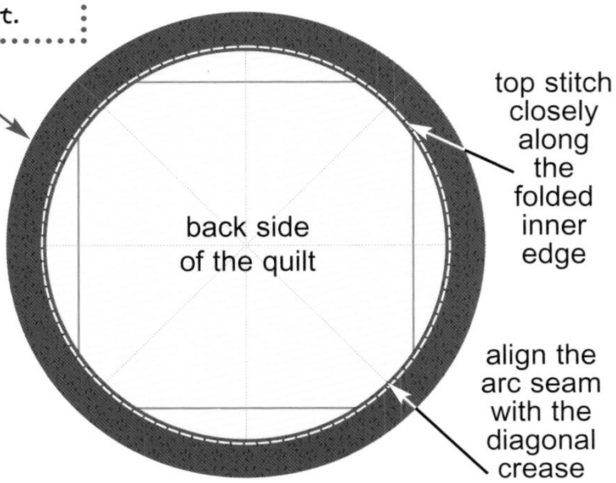
back side
of the quilt
top stitch closely along the folded inner edge
align the arc seam with the diagonal crease

Quilting

Marking Quilting Design Lines

- Trace a quilting line directly onto the 12 1/2" interior square. Two design options are found on page 54.
- Another option is to trace the design onto tear-away tracing paper, pin the paper to the square, and stitch through the paper.

7"
area where interior block fabric is visible

Layering with Basting Spray

- Lightly spray one side of the cotton batting.
- Center the batting square (sprayed side) on the wrong side of the interior square and pat to smooth the layers.
- Lightly spray the back side of the batting.
- Fold the corners an approximate 1/4" edge over the batting square, finger pressing the edge as you go.
- Place the interior square *(with batting)* right side up onto the wrong side of the backing circle.
  The marked guide line will be visible.
- The diagonal creases of the backing and the corner of the interior square should be aligned.
- Pat and smooth the layers together.

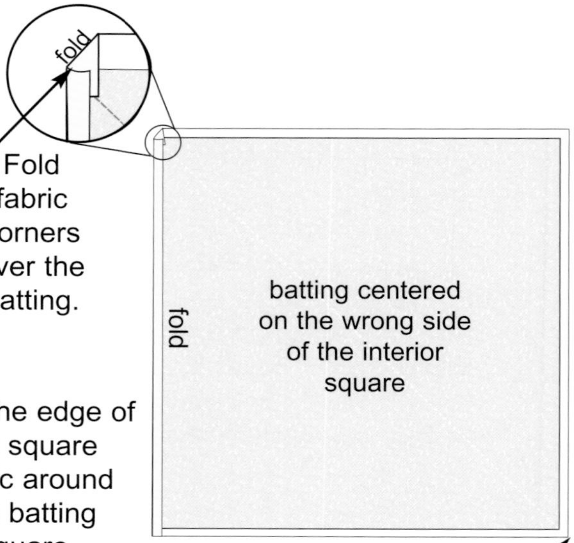
fold
Fold fabric corners over the batting.
fold
batting centered on the wrong side of the interior square
Fold the edge of the square fabric around the batting square.
1/2" of interior fabric extends around the batting

Layering with Hobbs Fusible Batting

- Center the batting on the wrong side of the interior square.
- Fold the corners of the interior square around the batting square and gently press. Use medium heat and just tap the corner down to hold it in place.
- Fold about 1/4" edge over the batting square, pressing the edge as you go.
- Place the interior square *(with batting)* right side up onto the wrong side of the backing circle.
  The marked guide line will be visible.
- The diagonal creases of the backing and the corner of the interior square should be aligned.
- Gently iron the layers together.

Quilting

- Quilt the layers by machine or hand along the lines of the marked quilting design.
- Sometimes your quilting can distort the block out of square. If this happens, gently steam press the layers to eliminate any excess fullness and smooth the circle.

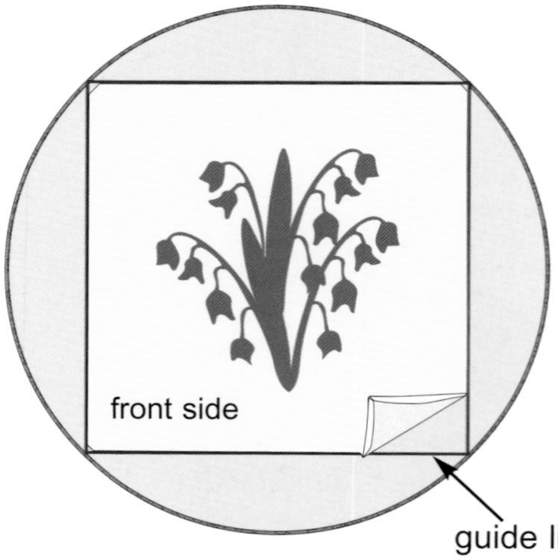
front side
guide line
Place the folded edges in line with the marked guide line, keeping the marked line visible.

Seamless Scallops

Scallop Definition

Scallops form the curved border of the quilt. Scallops are added to the outer blocks ***before*** the blocks are put together. The corner blocks have two scallops added, the side blocks have one scallop added. The outer edge of each scallop is finished with an arc piece, eliminating the need for traditional binding.

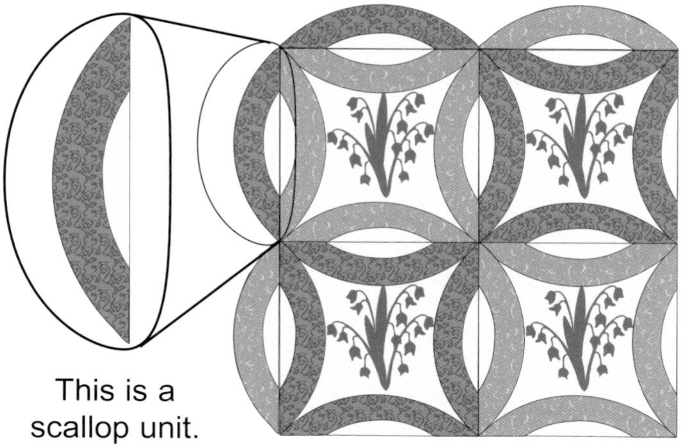
This is a
scallop unit.

Adding Scallops to Blocks

- Select the blocks which will have scallops added to them. They are the blocks on the outside of the quilt. See page 9 for block placement.
- Unfold the scallop piece.

working from the back

- Place the ***right*** side of the scallop onto the ***back*** side of the block. The corners of the scallop extend 1/4" beyond the backing circle on each side.
- Match the fold line to the marked guide line on the front side of the block.

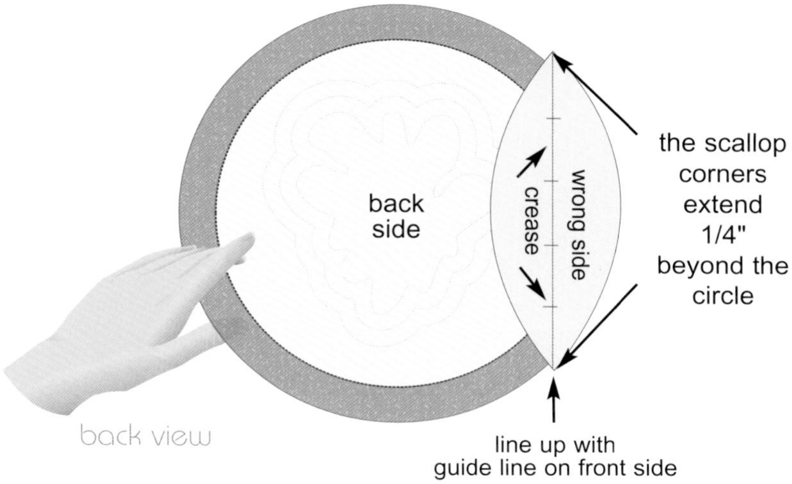
back
side
crease
wrong side
the scallop
corners
extend
1/4"
beyond the
circle
back view
line up with
guide line on front side

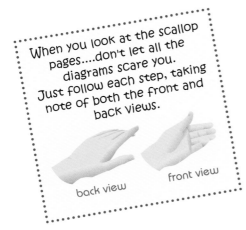

When you look at the scallop pages....don't let all the diagrams scare you. Just follow each step, taking note of both the front and back views.

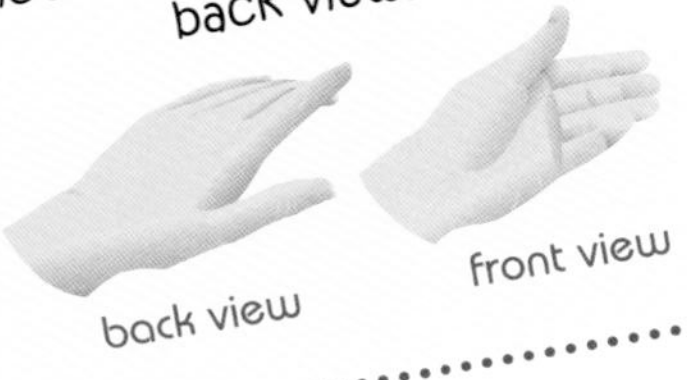
back view
front view

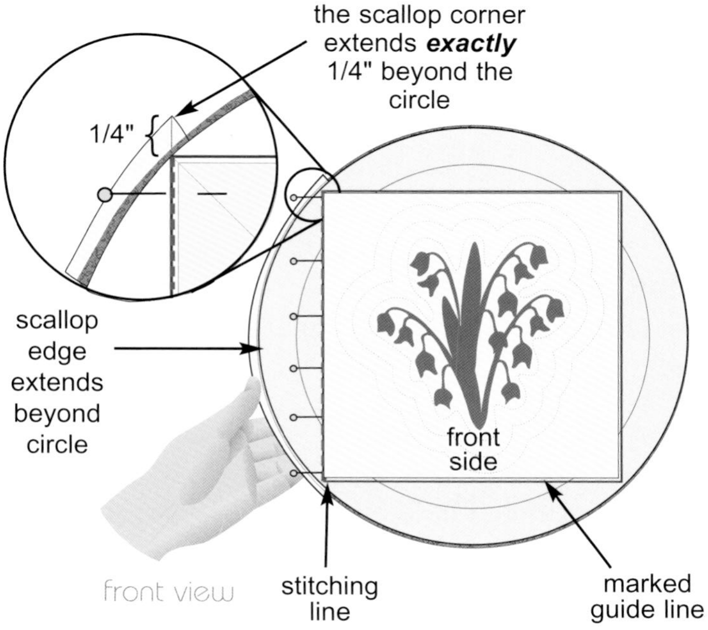
the scallop corner
extends ***exactly***
1/4" beyond the
circle
1/4"
scallop
edge
extends
beyond
circle
front
side
front view
stitching
line
marked
guide line

Sewing Scallops to Blocks

working from the front

- Pin the scallop to the circle, matching the marked guide line to the crease of the underlying scallop piece.
- Sew precisely along the guide line, back stitching to secure your stitches at the beginning and end of the seam.

Seamless Scallops

working from the front

- Pin the flap of the block to the interior square to keep it out of your way. Don't catch the scallop piece as you pin.

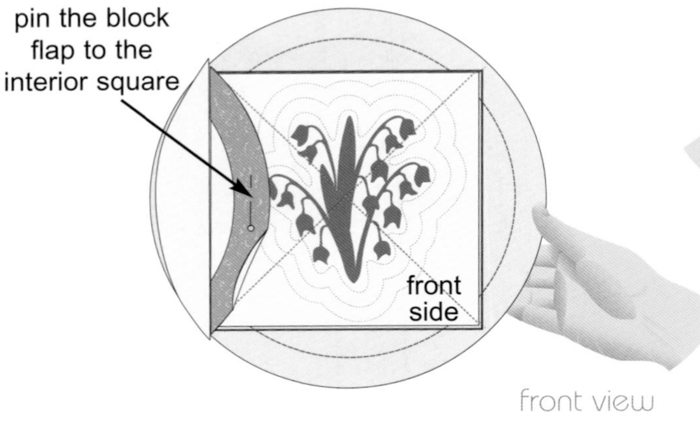

pin the block flap to the interior square
front side
front view

Adding an Arc to the Scallop

- Choose an arc of the opposite color family:
  Fabric B arcs to Fabric A circles.
  Fabric A arcs to Fabric B circles.
- Spray the arc with spray sizing. While wet, precisely fold under 1/4" along the inner curved edge.
- Press the fold being careful not to stretch the edge.

working from the back

- Pin the ***right*** side of an arc to the back side of the scallop edges, centering it with the scallop.

working from the front

- Match the end of the arc to the tip of the scallop.
- Stitch from the front side of block, beginning ***precisely*** at the point of intersection, back stitching to secure the stitches at the beginning and end of the seam.

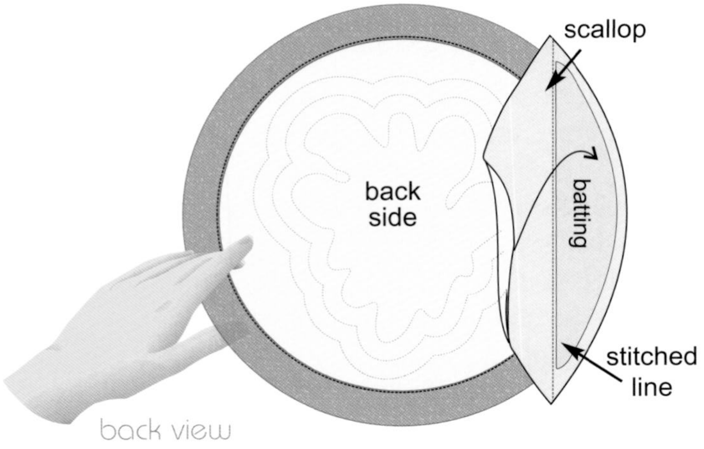

scallop
back side
batting
stitched line
back view

Adding Batting to the Scallop

working from the back

- Center the batting on the scallop even with the stitched line.
- Fold the scallop halves together.
- Pin the edges of the scallop together with the batting between the layers.

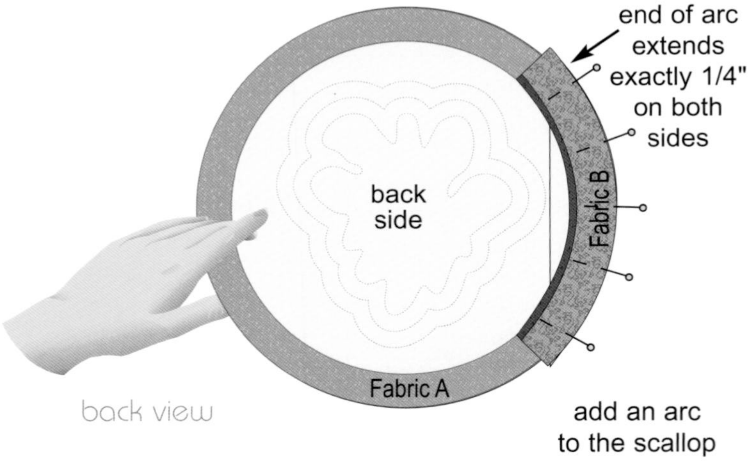

end of arc extends exactly 1/4" on both sides
back side
Fabric B
Fabric A
back view
add an arc to the scallop

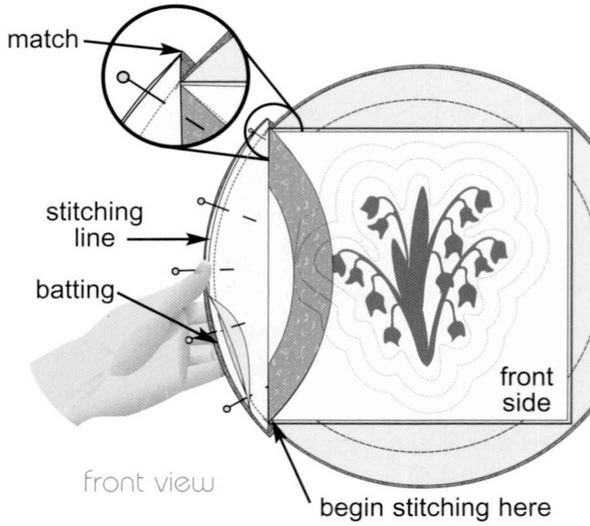

match
stitching line
batting
front side
front view
begin stitching here

Seamless Scallops

working from the back

- Fold the corners of the arc even with the seam joining the scallop to the block.
- Finger press this fold line. You may need to adjust this fold slightly when you bring it over to the other side.

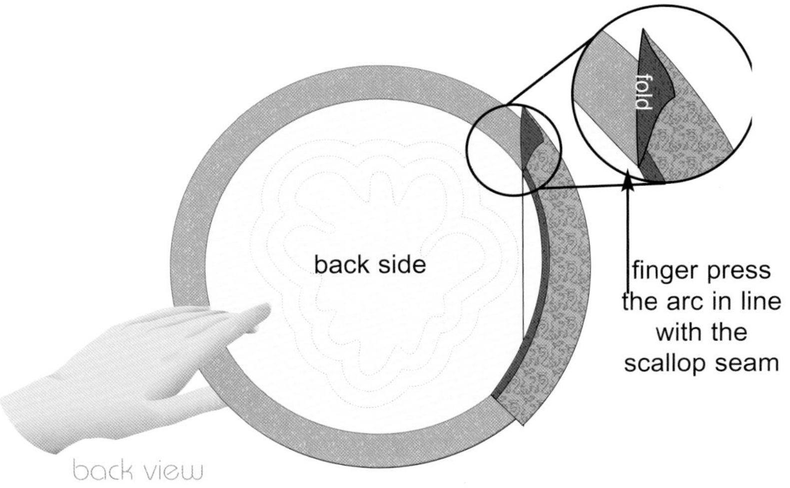

fold
back side
finger press the arc in line with the scallop seam
back view

working from the front

- Bring the arc over the scallop edge to the front side of the block.
- Wrap the corner of the arc around the seam as shown.
- There are several ways to secure the "ear", *(that tiny corner of fabric),* by hand sewing, finger rolling, or using a stiletto. Details of the hand stitching method are as follows:
  - Using a milliner's needle and matching thread, hide the knot in the seam allowance.
  - To reduce the bulk of fabric, fold the scallop "ear" to the front and the arc "ear" toward the back.
  - Hand sew several stitches to hold the folded "ears".
- Trim fabric ***only*** if necessary.

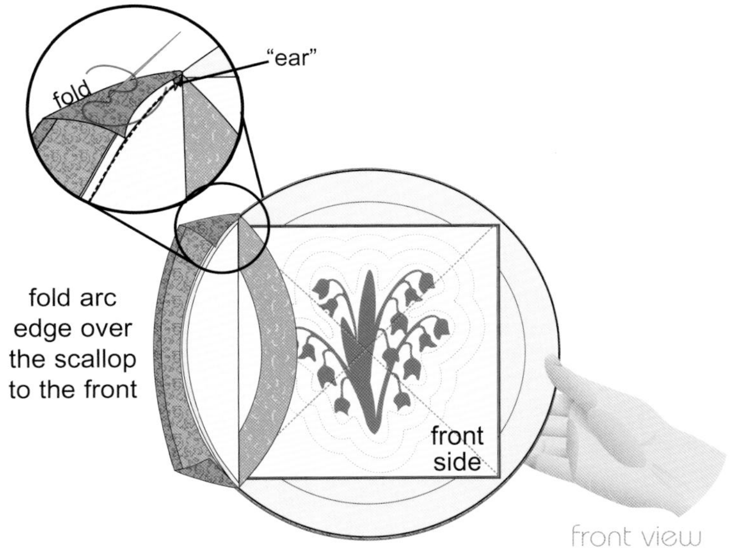

fold
"ear"
fold arc edge over the scallop to the front
front side
front view

- Match the arcs and pin, keeping the threaded needle out of the way.
- Pin the folded edge of the arc to the scallop.
- Hand stitch the folded edge to the arc. Use an invisible stitch to hide your stitches.
- Top stitch along the inner edge of the arc.
- Repeat the steps for the remaining scallops.

Note: Corner blocks will have two scallops added.

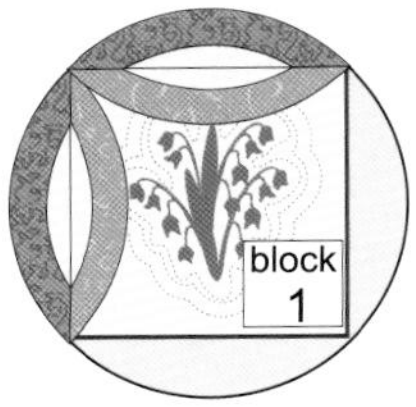

block 1

corner block label "block 1"

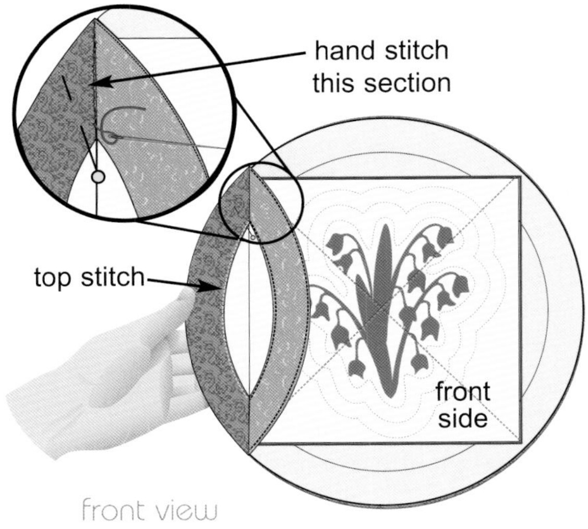

hand stitch this section
top stitch
front side
front view

Assembling Seamless Wedding Ring Blocks

A nine block quilt is shown for assembling blocks.

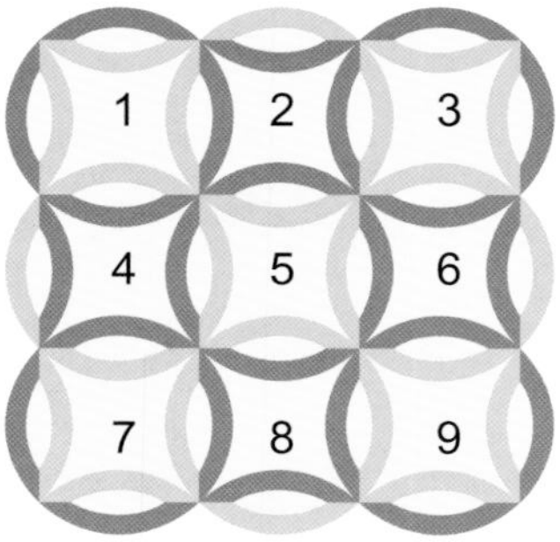
1
2
3
4
5
6
7
8
9

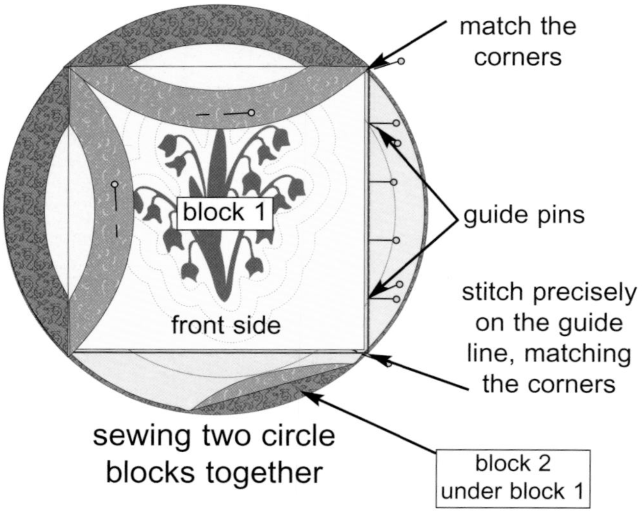
match the corners
block 1
guide pins
front side
stitch precisely on the guide line, matching the corners
sewing two circle blocks together
block 2 under block 1

Sewing the Block Pairs

- Place a Block A on top of a block B, with the back sides together.
- Match the guide lines of both blocks.
- Place a pin where the arcs intersect with the guide line.
- Using this pin as a guide, match the corresponding point in the block below.
- Add a second pin to hold this match point securely, leaving the guide pin in its position.
- Repeat for the other point.
- Pin along the guide line, matching it to the guide line of the circle block below. Be sure you pin the edge of the blocks, again matching the guidelines.
- Baste along the marked line and check for accuracy.

Basting will save you time in the long run. Adjustments will be much easier. Just use your longest machine stitching, then just stitch over the top when you know you've got it right.

Before Top stitching...
The best way to beat the bulk is to cinch the corner together using a short stiff hand needle and strong thread. Put only a couple of stitches here--no more than 1/4" into the block. You may also cinch together the ends of the scallops if needed.

- Once you've determined the seam is correct, reset your machine stitching to a shorter stitch length for strength.
- Stitch precisely along the guide line, back stitching to secure your stitches at the beginning and end of the seam.

Top Stitching the Rings

- Pin each flap to each interior square, centering the arc edge with the diagonal fold line of the square. Be sure each flap is nice and smooth before top stitching. Check the back for tucks or wrinkles.
- Top stitch along the outer edge of the arc, securing it to the block.
- Top stitch at each stage of assembly.

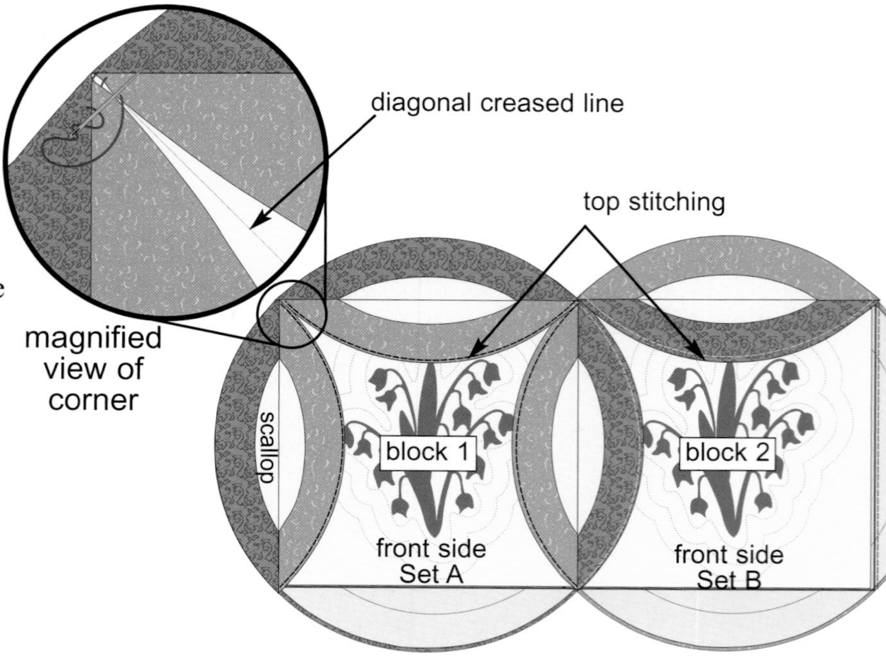
diagonal creased line
top stitching
magnified view of corner
scallop
block 1
block 2
front side Set A
front side Set B

Assembling Seamless Wedding Ring Blocks

Sewing the Block Foursome

- Place two block pairs together, with back sides together. Notice the rings will be opposite color families.
- Match the guide lines of both blocks.
- Place a pin where each arc intersects the guide line.
- Using this pin as a guide, match the corresponding point in the block below.
- Add a second pin to hold the match point securely, leaving the guide pin in its position.

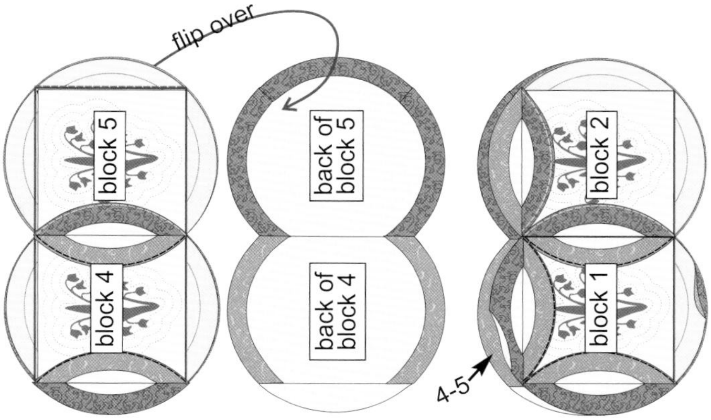
flip over
block 5
block 4
back of block 5
back of block 4
block 2
block 1
4-5
front side of **4-5** block pair
back side of **4-5** block pair
put block pair 1-2 on top of pair 4-5, back sides facing

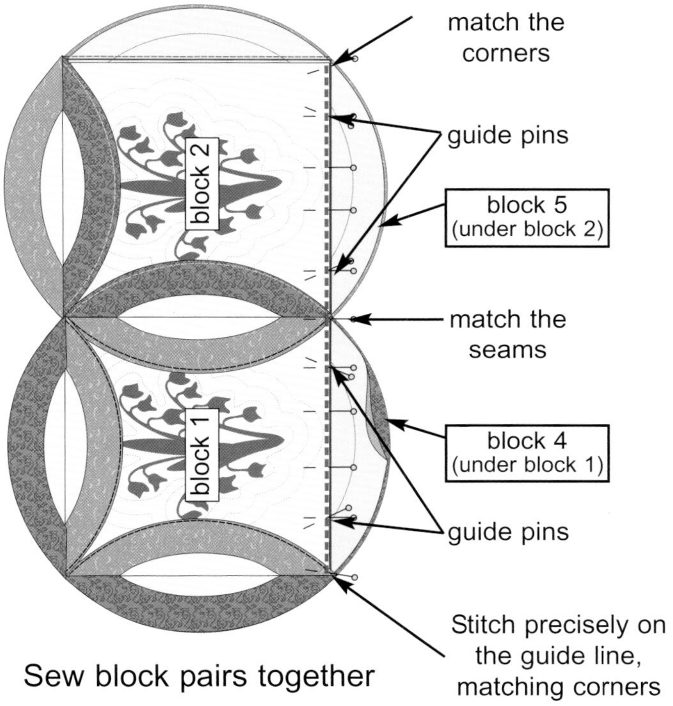
match the corners
guide pins
block 2
block 5 (under block 2)
match the seams
block 1
block 4 (under block 1)
guide pins
Stitch precisely on the guide line, matching corners

Sew block pairs together

- Pin along the guide line, matching it to the guide line of the circle blocks below. Be sure the intersection of each block pair matches as well.
- Stitch precisely along the guide line, back stitching to secure your stitches at the beginning and end of the seam.

- Open the flaps of each block of the **1-2-4-5** foursome.
- Pin the flaps to the interior square, centering the arcs with the diagonal fold line of the square. Be sure both sides of your quilt are nice and smooth before top stitching.

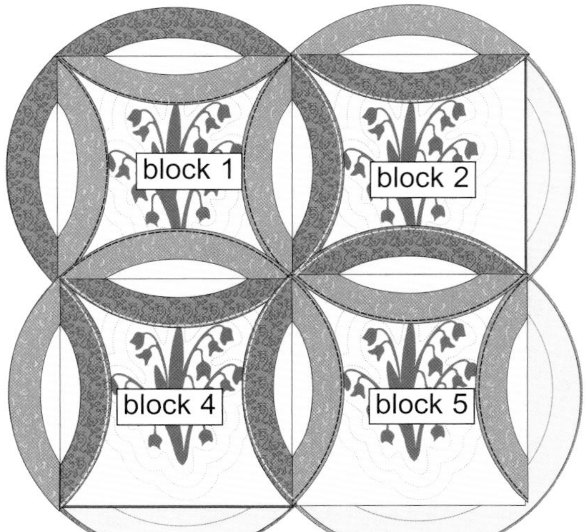
block 1
block 2
block 4
block 5

1-2-4-5 block foursome

Cinch the corner together using a short stiff quilting or between needle and strong thread using a couple of stitches (no more than 1/4" into the block).

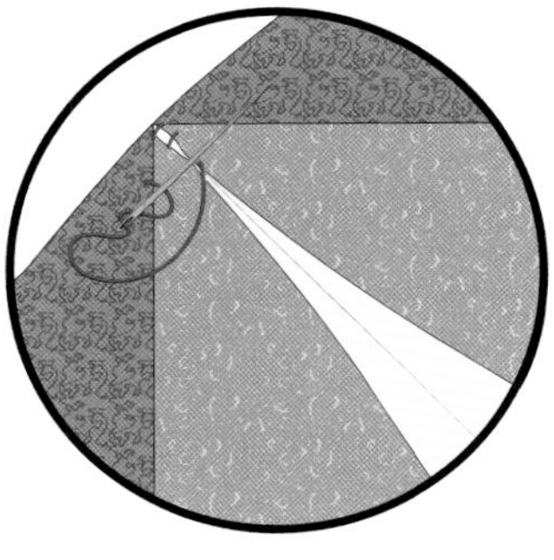

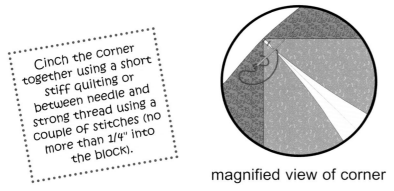

magnified view of corner

- Top stitch along the outer edge of the arc, securing it to the block.
- Top stitch at each stage of assembly.

Assembling Seamless Wedding Ring Blocks

- Sew blocks **3** and **6** together to make a block pair.
- Sew the **1-2-4-5** foursome to the **3-6** block pair.
- Open the flaps of each block and pin to the interior square, centering the arcs with the diagonal fold line. Smooth before top stitching.
- Top stitch along the outer edge of the arc, securing it to the block.
- Alternatives to top stitching include blind stitching with monofilament (clear) thread, decorative stitching with contrasting thread, or adding trim to cover the top stitching.

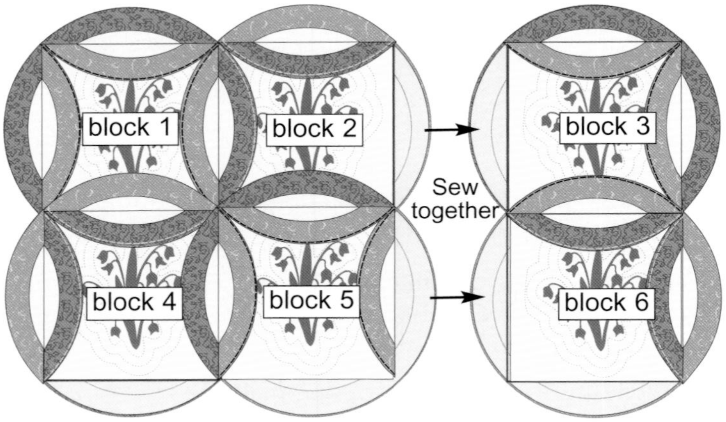

block 1
block 2
block 3
Sew together
block 4
block 5
block 6

1-2-4-5 block foursome   **3-6** block pair

- Sew blocks **7** to **8** to make a block pair.
- Sew block **9** to the **7-8** pair.
- Sew the **1-2-3-4-5-6** set to the **7-8-9** set.
- Open the flaps of each block and pin to the interior square, centering each arc with the diagonal fold line. Be sure both sides of your quilt are nice and smooth before top stitching.
- Top stitch along the outer edge of the flap, securing it to the block.

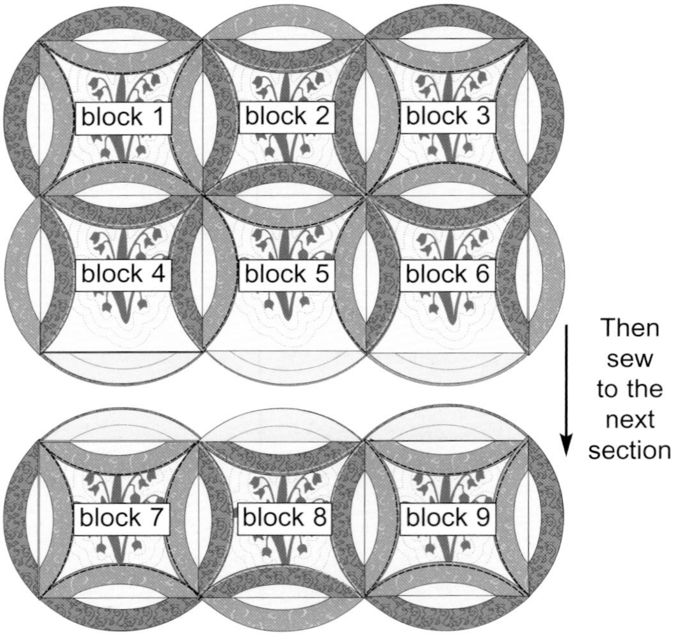

block 1
block 2
block 3
block 4
block 5
block 6
Then sew to the next section
block 7
block 8
block 9

When you've sewn the blocks together...

You're done!

No binding or quilting left to do.

Yeah!

Your wedding ring is now finished.

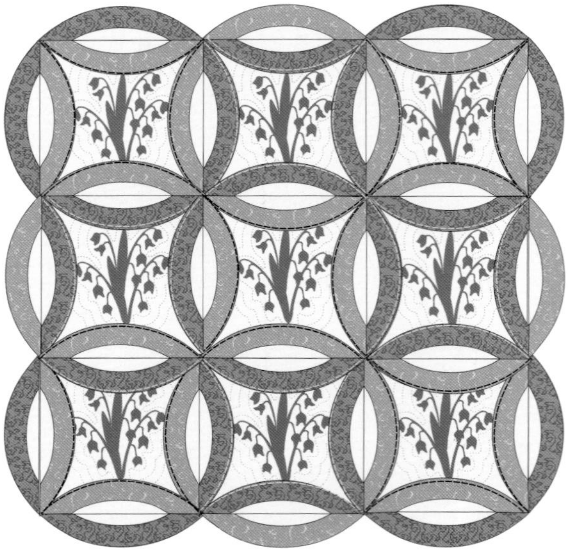

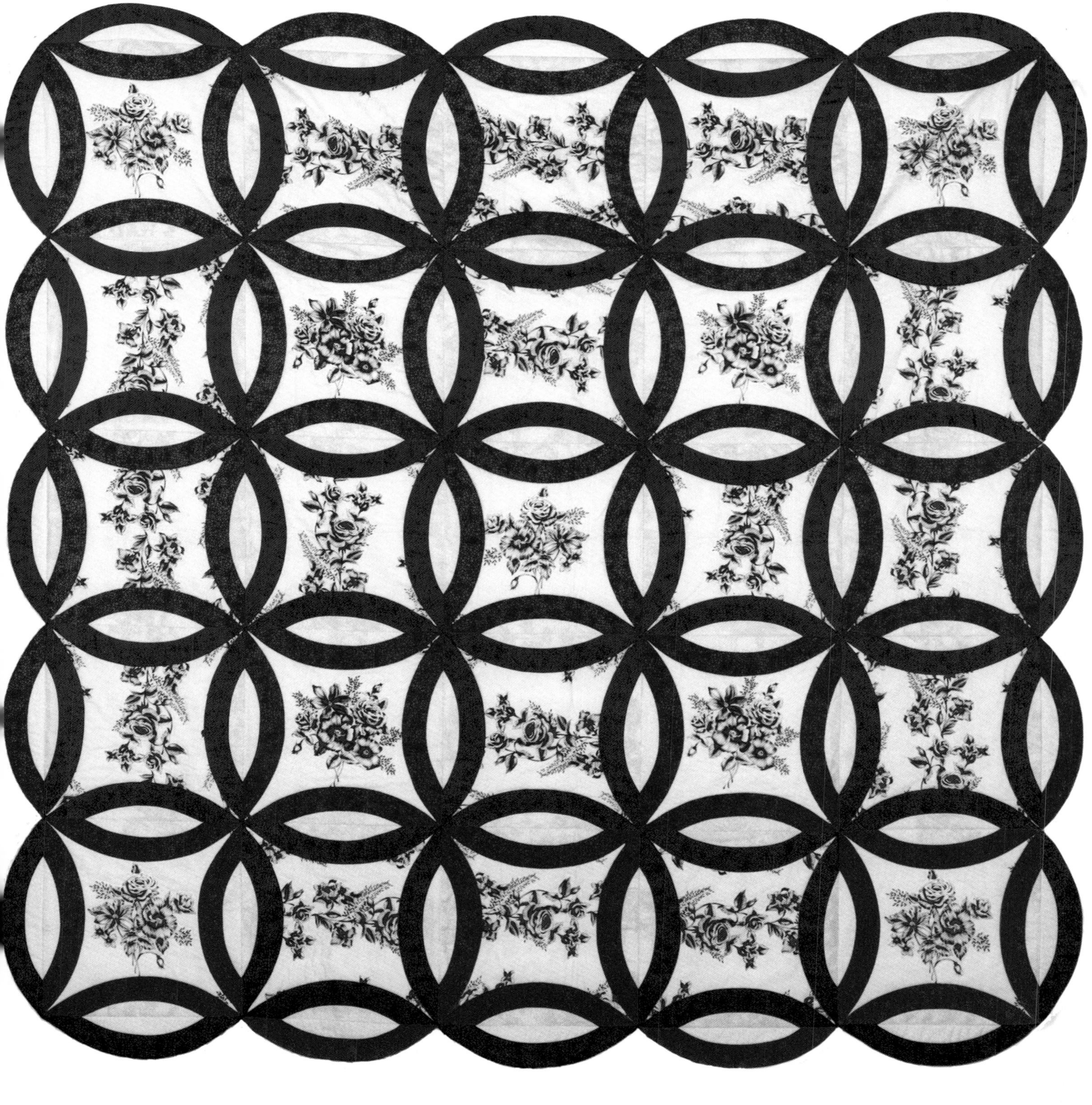

Fine China Blue

interlocking rings of china blue

fabric from the Porcelain Collectibles Line
by Northcott Inc.

Rose Garden

colors give a romantic look to traditional blocks
appliqued rose blocks on a two tone background

Victorian Wedding

crazy pieced squares
embellished
with buttons
and bits of lace

Trapunto Elegance

light dances across the satin in the block centers

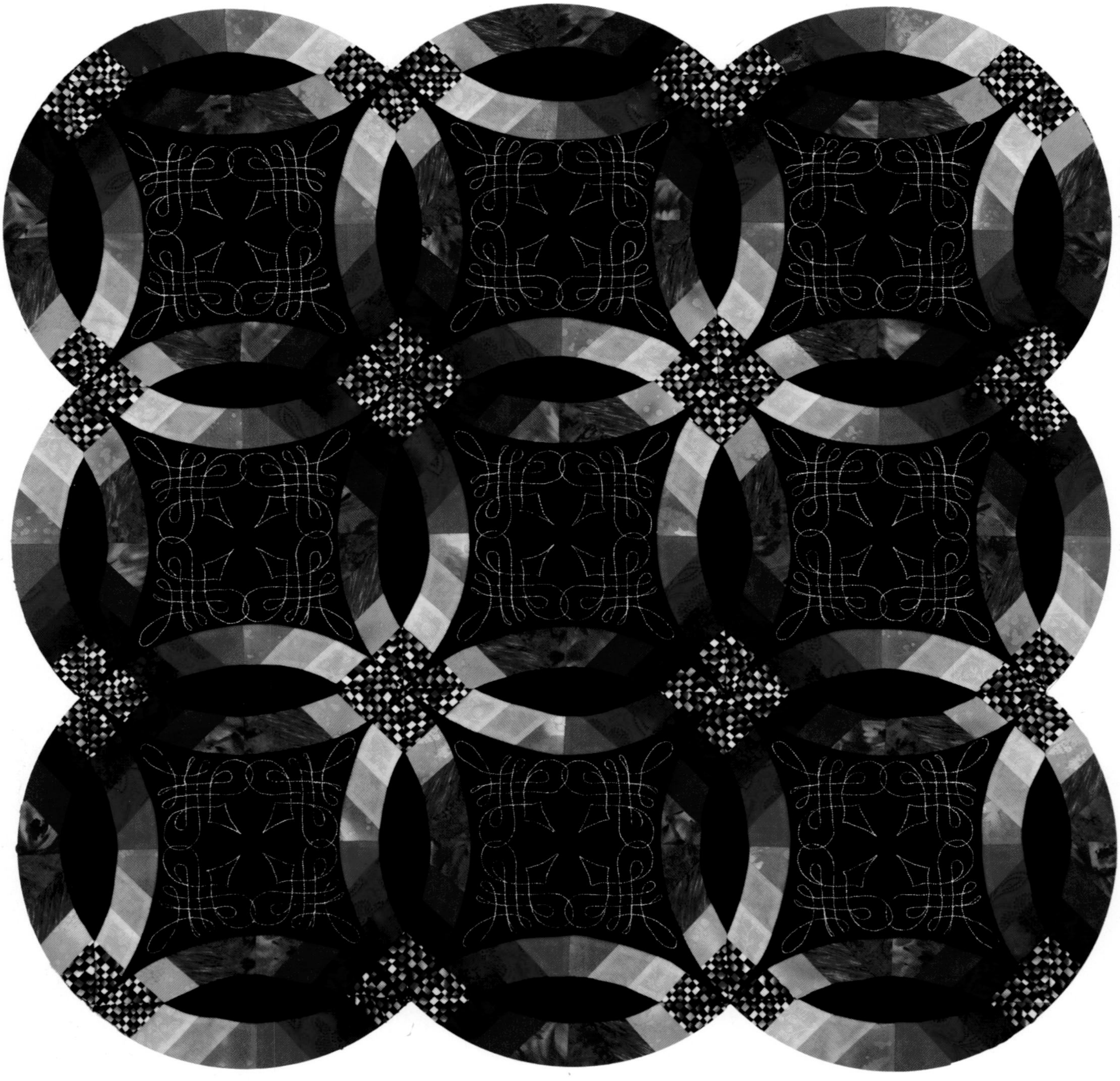

The Rainbow

interlocking color wheels
quilted with verigated metallic thread

Four Seasons of Wedding Rings...

Fall
harvest leaves
and grapes
appliqued over a
braided bias vine

Spring
painted lilacs
with stippled petals on the
gentle soft greens of spring

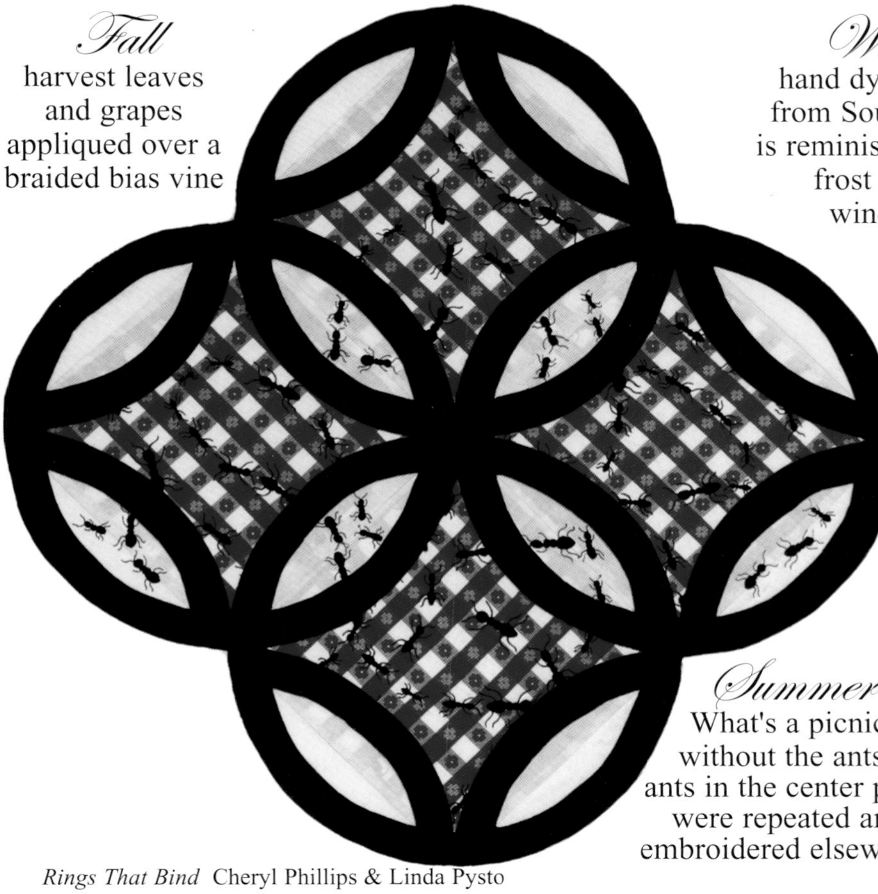

Summer
What's a picnic
without the ants?
ants in the center print
were repeated and
embroidered elsewhere

Winter
hand dyed fabric
from South Africa
is reminiscent of the
frost on the
windows

East meets West

Imperial Wedding

The pieced back is as intriguing as the front

Chinese characters
for love and the four winds
are quilted into the blocks

various arc fabrics add interest

Home on the Range

Rings of woodgrain fabric frame
colorful characters from the old west

hand painted blocks
by Donna Reppo

The Salsa

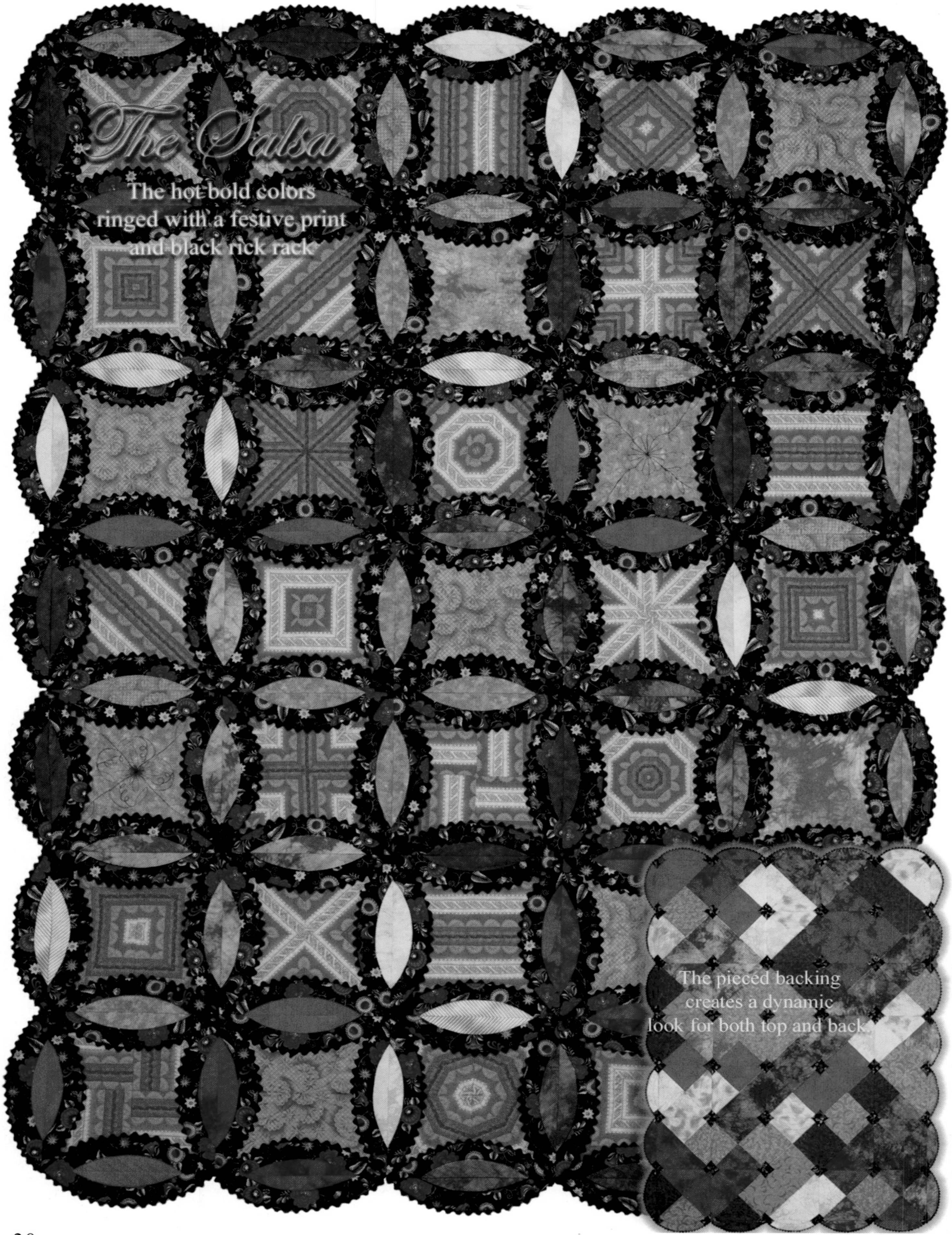

The hot bold colors ringed with a festive print and black rick rack

The pieced backing creates a dynamic look for both top and back.

Striped Fabric

Whether it's a border stripe or an awning stripe, both give the look of complexity with half the effort!

Lake House Trellis

lovely toile fabric from
Lake House Fabrics
seamless arcs are made from a
coordinating stripe

Lake House Blues

floral fabric from
Lake House Fabrics
is framed with arcs
of geometric stripe

COOKIES

She's a Thirties Girl

Pieced arcs of reproduction fabric
frame nostalgic embroidered designs.
The embroidery doubles as the quilting.

Cutting Backing

Backing Circles	18" Squares	Single 1	Runner 1 x 3	Wall 2 x 2	Baby 3 x 3	Lap 5 x 5	Twin 5 x 7	Double 6 x 7	Queen 7 x 8	King 8 x 8
	Backing Circles	1	3	4	9	25	35	42	56	64

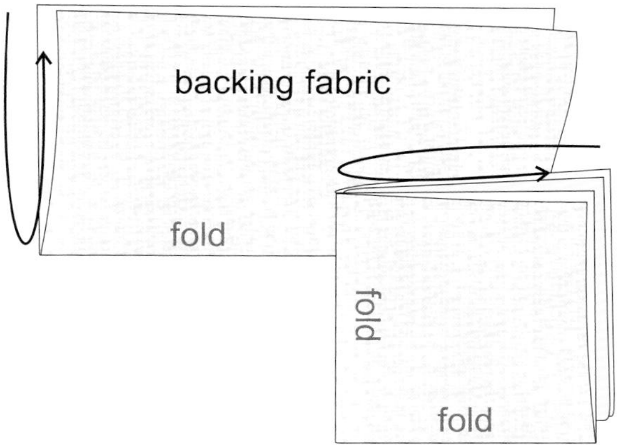

backing fabric
fold
fold
fold

Cutting the Backing

- Cut 18" squares as listed above for your quilt size.
- Test your fabric square for shrinkage. See page 6 for more fabric concerns.

  Fold the square into quarters:
  - Fold in half.
  - Press the fold.
  - Fold in half again.
  - Press the new fold.

Time Saving Tip

Reduce the bulk of a large piece of fabric by first tearing it into squares. Don't worry about the torn edges as you'll be cutting them off in the next step.

- First, clip the selvage and tear to establish the grain.
- Measure 18" along the selvage and clip a notch. Tear the piece crosswise.
- Notch the strip in 18" increments, tear two squares, and iron.
- Repeat for the number of background circles needed.

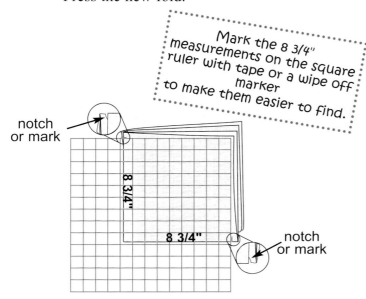

Mark the 8 3/4" measurements on the square ruler with tape or a wipe off marker to make them easier to find.

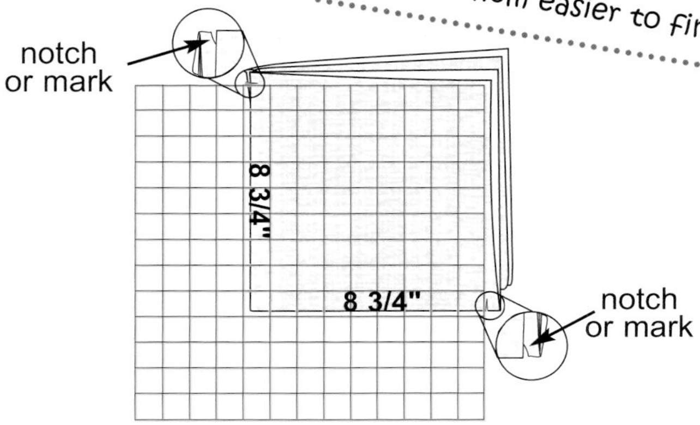

notch
or mark
8 3/4"
8 3/4"
notch
or mark

- Place a square ruler on the folded backing, aligning both 8 3/4" marks with the folded sides.
- Cut little notches, or mark to establish these points.

Cutting the Backing into Circles

- Place the Arc-Ease tool onto the folded fabric, aligning marked edge of the tool ***precisely*** with both 8 3/4" notches.
- Cut the square along the outer edge of the Arc-Ease tool into a circle.
- Measure the circle to be sure it's truly round and the diameter is exactly 17 1/2".

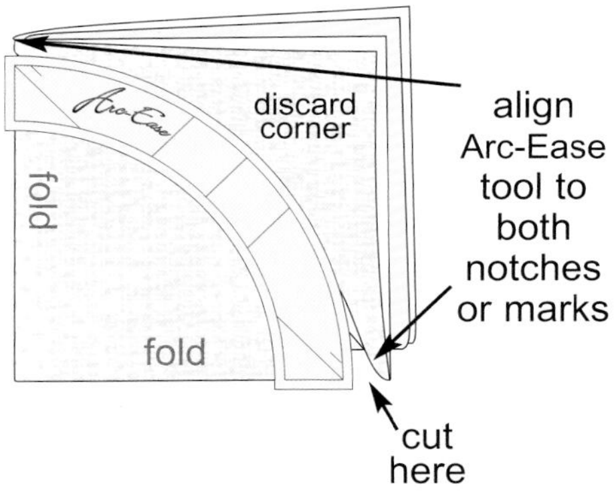

discard
corner
fold
fold
align
Arc-Ease
tool to
both
notches
or marks
cut
here

Cutting for the Pieced Arc Wedding Ring

Interior Squares

Interior Squares	Single 1	Runner 1 x 3	Wall 2 x 2	Baby 3 x 3	Lap 5 x 5	Twin 5 x 7	Double 6 x 7	Queen 7 x 8	King 8 x 8
12 1/2" Squares	1	3	4	9	25	35	42	56	64

Cutting the Interior Squares

- Cut squares of interior fabric, referring to the chart above .
- Complete any applique or embroidery intended for the interior square before layering.
    - The applique pattern as seen on the front cover can be found on page 55.
    - Creative options for your interior squares can be found on page 46.

interior
square

Scallops

Scallops cut from 6 x 13" Strips of backing fabric	Single 1	Runner 1 x 3	Wall 2 x 2	Baby 3 x 3	Lap 5 x 5	Twin 5 x 7	Double 6 x 7	Queen 7 x 8	King 8 x 8
Total Number of Scallops	4	8	8	12	20	24	26	30	32

Cutting the Scallops

- Fold the 6" x 13" strip of backing fabric in half lengthwise with wrong sides together and press the fold.
- Place the Arc-Ease tool on the fabric, so that the horizontal lines are directly on the fold.
- Cut *only* along the outside edge of the Arc-Ease tool.
- Cut the number of scallops as listed in the chart above.

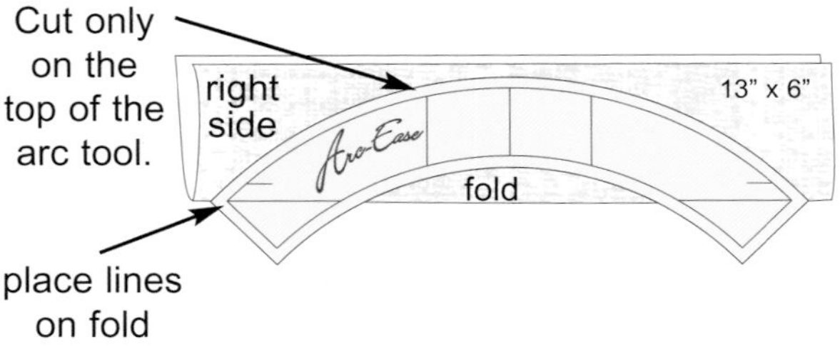
Cut only
on the
top of the
arc tool.
right
side
13" x 6"
fold
place lines
on fold

Batting

Batting	Single 1	Runner 1 x 3	Wall 2 x 2	Baby 3 x 3	Lap 5 x 5	Twin 5 x 7	Double 6 x 7	Queen 7 x 8	King 8 x 8
11 1/2" Squares	1	3	4	9	25	35	42	56	64
Scallops	4	8	8	12	20	24	26	30	32

Cutting the Batting

- Referring to the chart, cut the 11 1/2" squares.
- To cut scallops of batting, place the Arc-Ease tool on batting with a straight edge of the batting lining up with the short lines on the arc tool.
- Cut *only* along the outside edge of the Arc-Ease tool.
- Trim the corners of the batting scallops.
- Set aside the scallop pieces for later use.

batting
for block

Cut 11 1/2" squares.

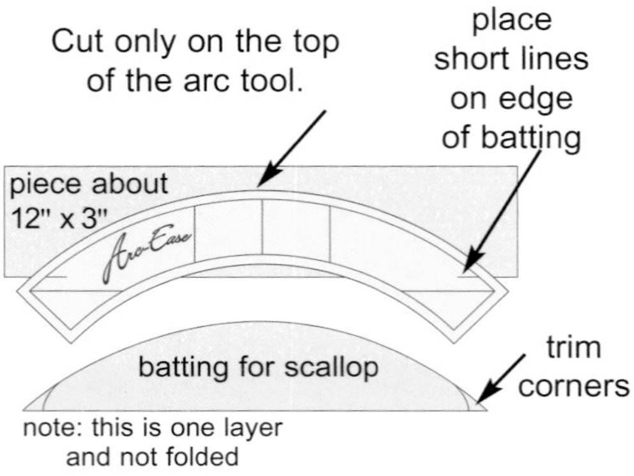
Cut only on the top
of the arc tool.
place
short lines
on edge
of batting
piece about
12" x 3"
batting for scallop
trim
corners
note: this is one layer
and not folded

Cutting Pieced Arcs

Strips

Strips cut across width	Single 1	Runner 1 x 3	Wall 2 x 2	Baby 3 x 3	Lap 5 x 5	Twin 5 x 7	Double 6 x 7	Queen 7 x 8	King 8 x 8
2 1/2" wide strips D-1, C-1 C-2, D-2	1 each	1 each	1 each	2 each	5 each	7 each	9 each	11 each	12 each
1 3/4" wide strips E-1, F-1. A-1,B-1 E-2, F-2, A-2, B-2	1 each	1 each	1 each	2 each	5 each	7 each	9 each	11 each	12 each
2 1/4" wide strips S-1*, S-2*	2 each	2 each	2 each	4 each	10 each	14 each	18 each	22 each	24 each

*Note: both S fabrics are used in each strip set.

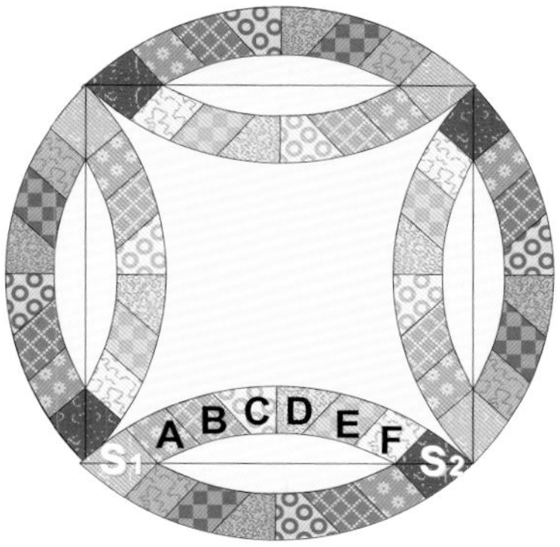

A
B
C
D
E
F
S1
S2

D-1	2 1/2"
E-1	1 3/4"
F-1	1 3/4"
S-2	2 1/4"
S-1	2 1/4"
A-1	1 3/4"
B-1	1 3/4"
C-1	2 1/2"

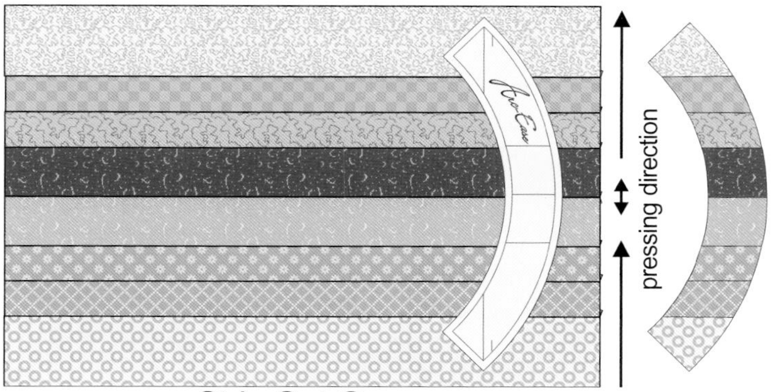

Arc-Ease
pressing direction

Strip Set One

D-2	2 1/2"
E-2	1 3/4"
F-2	1 3/4"
S-1	2 1/4"
S-2	2 1/4"
A-2	1 3/4"
B-2	1 3/4"
C-2	2 1/2"

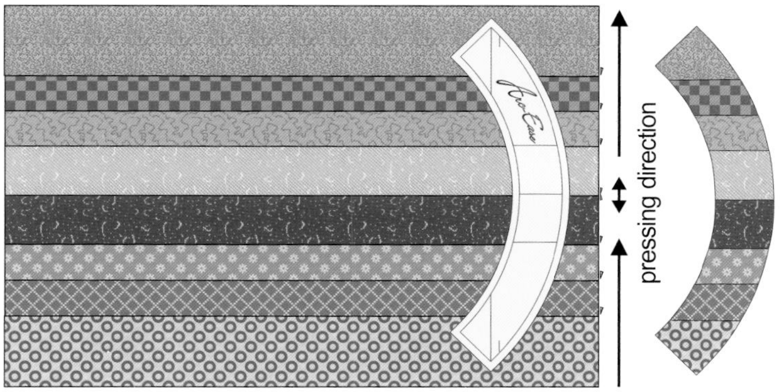

Arc-Ease
pressing direction

Strip Set Two

Be careful to keep the strips in order.

When you select fabrics, keep in mind the S fabrics go in the corners of the block, and the C and D fabrics come together in the center of the arc.

Cutting Strips

- Cut strips for each color family.

Sewing Strip Sets

- Sew with ***exact*** 1/4" seams, 18-20 stitches per inch (1.5 to 2).
- Sew the strips to make **Strip Set One** in the order listed above.
- Sew the strips to make **Strip Set Two** in the order listed above.
- Press the strip sets from the back as indicated by the arrows above. The S-S seam is pressed open.

Cutting Arcs

- Prepare the Arc-Ease tool by applying loops of wide transparent packaging tape, sticky side out, to the back side of the tool. This will keep the Arc-Ease tool from slipping, assuring an accurate cut.
- Consistently place the strip set right side up with fabric D to the top and the Arc-Ease tool curving right.
- Placing the *Arc-Ease* tool onto the strip set with the center line on the S-S seam line and the other seams parallel, cut the number of arcs as listed for your quilt size in the chart on the top of the next page.

Pieced Rings

Arcs

Pieced Arc Version	Single 1	Runner 1 x 3	Wall 2 x 2	Baby 3 x 3	Lap 5 x 5	Twin 5 x 7	Double 6 x 7	Queen 7 x 8	King 8 x 8
Total Arcs	8	20	24	48	120	164	194	254	288
Set One and Set Two Arcs	4 each	10 each	12 each	24 each	60 each	82 each	97 each	127 each	144 each
Set One Arcs for Scallops	0	2	4	4	8	10	13	15	16
Set Two Arcs for Scallops	4	6	4	8	12	14	13	15	16

Making Rings

- Set aside arcs for later use with scallops.
- Place two arcs together, right sides facing, with the C-1 Fabric on top of the D-1 Fabric.
- Sew the arcs together to make a pair. Sew with ***exact*** 1/4" seams.
- Sew two arc pairs together to make a ring.
- Press the seams joining the arcs open.
- Spray the arc with spray sizing. While wet, precisely fold under 1/4" along the inner curved edge.
- Press the fold from the wrong side being careful not to stretch the edge.
- Refer to the chart below and make the number of rings listed for the quilt size you've selected.
- Repeat for Strip Set Two.

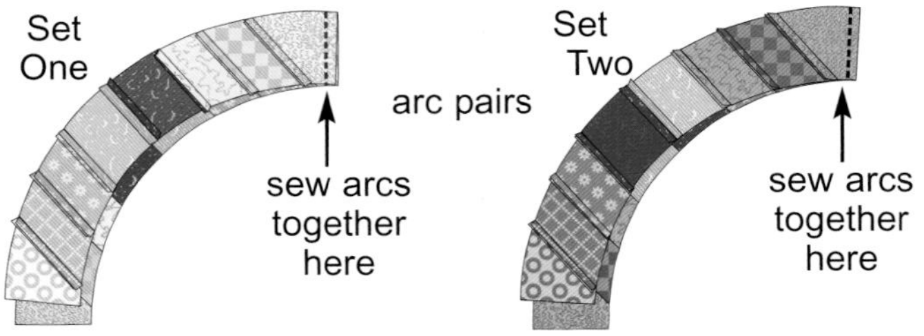

Set One
Set Two
arc pairs
sew arcs together here
sew arcs together here

Here's a trick to make the folded edge smooth and even. Stitch a scant 1/4" (less than) from the inner edge before folding to use as a pressing guide. This is similar to stay stitching used in clothing construction.

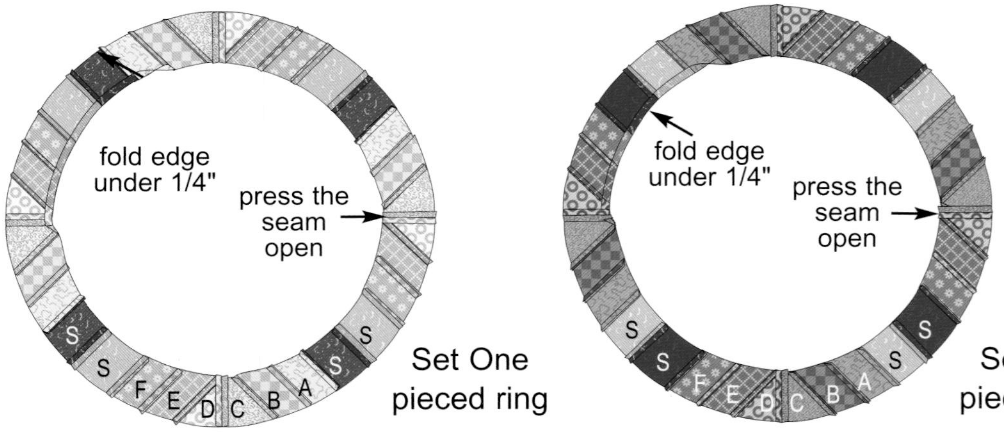

fold edge under 1/4"
press the seam open
S
S
S
S
F
E
D
C
B
A
fold edge under 1/4"
press the seam open
S
S
S
S
F
E
D
C
B
A

Set One pieced ring

Set Two pieced ring

Another Hint: Spray sizing will help hold the folded edge in place.

Rings

Pieced Version	Single 1	Runner 1 x 3	Wall 2 x 2	Baby 3 x 3	Lap 5 x 5	Twin 5 x 7	Double 6 x 7	Queen 7 x 8	King 8 x 8
Total Rings	1	3	4	9	25	35	42	56	64
Set One Rings	1	2	2	5	13	18	21	28	32
Set Two Rings	0	1	2	4	12	17	21	28	32

Backing Circles

- Open and refold the circle diagonally to establish precise eighth sections.
- Press the folds into creases. The creases will be used later for placement.

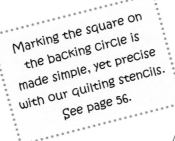

Marking the square on the backing circle is made simple, yet precise with our quilting stencils. See page 56.

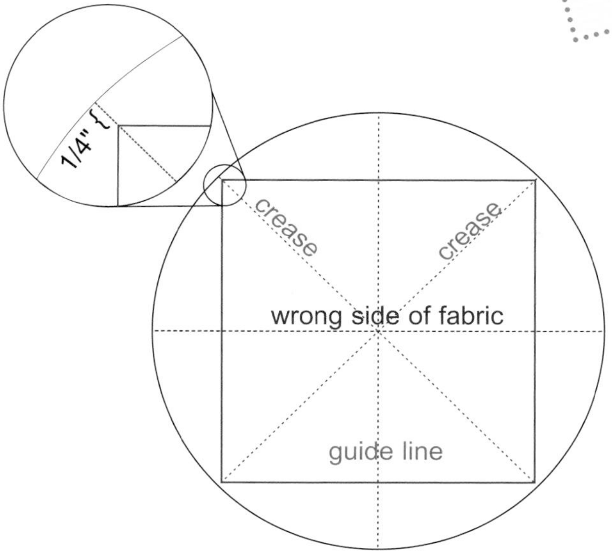

1/4"
crease
crease
wrong side of fabric
guide line

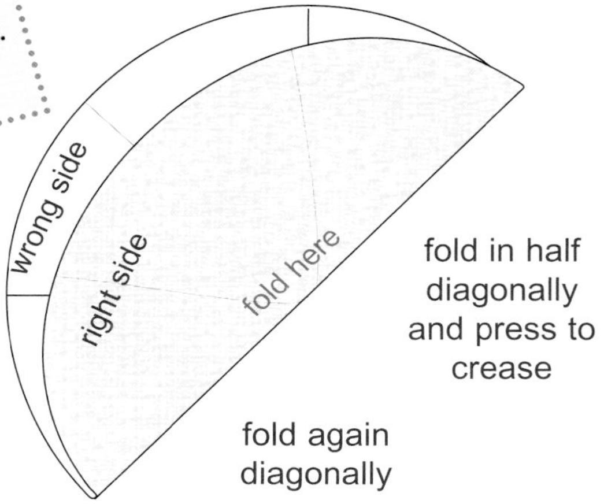

wrong side
right side
fold here
fold in half diagonally and press to crease
fold again diagonally

Marking the Backing Circle

- Measure along the diagonal crease 1/4" from the edge.
- Place a small dot at this point.
- Connecting the dots, draw a 12" square on the wrong side of the backing circle, with the corners of the square 1/4" from the edge of the circle and along the diagonal crease.
- Be sure you mark the lines of the square accurately. You'll be stitching along these guide lines when you sew the blocks together.

Sewing Pieced Rings to the Backing Circles

- Place the ***right*** side of the ring onto the ***wrong*** side of the backing circle.
- Match the S-S seam to the diagonal crease line.
- Match the seams joining the arcs to the circle creases.
- Pin the ring to the circle, with raw edges even.
- Sew the ring to the circle, stitching ***exactly*** 1/4" from the edge. The stitching through the S-S seam should intersect precisely with the corner of the marked square.

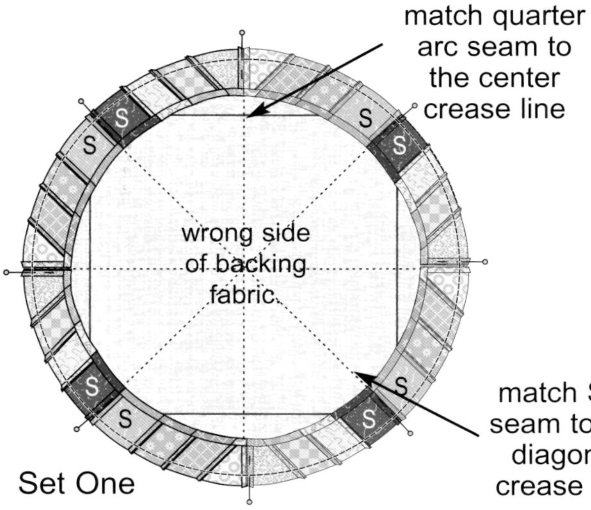

match quarter arc seam to the center crease line
S
S
S
S
S
S
S
S
wrong side of backing fabric
match S-S seam to the diagonal crease line

Set One

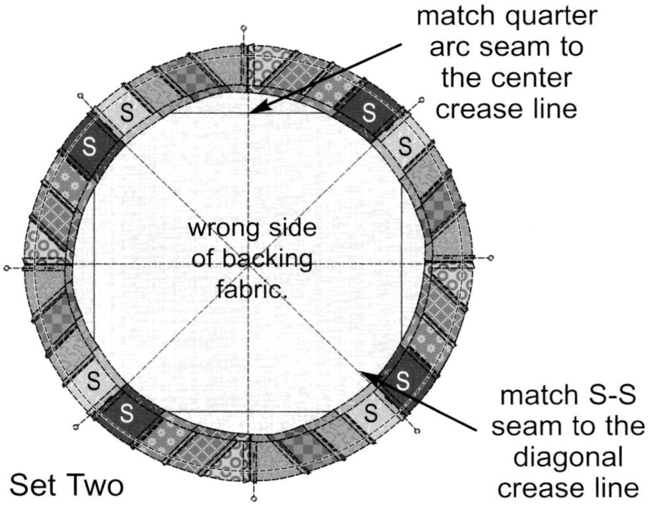

match quarter arc seam to the center crease line
S
S
S
S
S
S
S
S
wrong side of backing fabric
match S-S seam to the diagonal crease line

Set Two

Top Stitching Pieced Rings

Turning the Ring

- Grade the seam.
- Holding your scissors nearly flat, trim the seam allowance slightly.

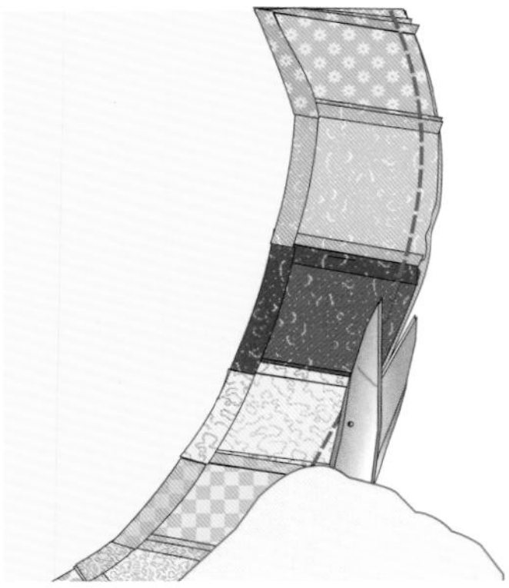

- Here are two suggestions to give a smooth edge and help eliminate any tucks along the curved edge.
  - Finger press the arc seam, smoothing the seam allowances toward the circle and away from the arc.
  - Stitch close to the circle seam on the side of the backing circle. The stitching goes through both seam allowances, in a similar manner to ***under stitching*** used in clothing

Think of the ring as a facing.

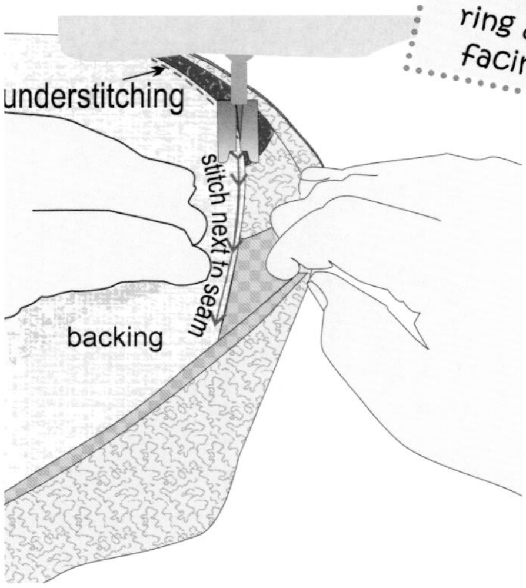
understitching
stitch next to seam
backing

- Bring the ring around the backing circle.
- Place a pin at the S-A seam through to the marked guide line on the other side.
- Repeat for the S-F seam.
- When aligned, pin the ring in place at each crease line, matching seams to creases, keeping the folded edge of the ring parallel to the outer edge of the circle.
- Press the ring in place.

Before stitching down the ring: Examine your circle. Is the arc the same width all the way around?

Top Stitching the Rings

- Top stitch very close to the folded inner edge .
- The top stitching is also called edge stitching. Sew approximately 1/16" from the folded edge. It is often helpful to lengthen the stitch for a smooth stitching line.
- Alternatives to top stitching include blind stitching with monofilament (clear) thread, decorative stitching with contrasting thread, or adding trim to cover the top stitching.

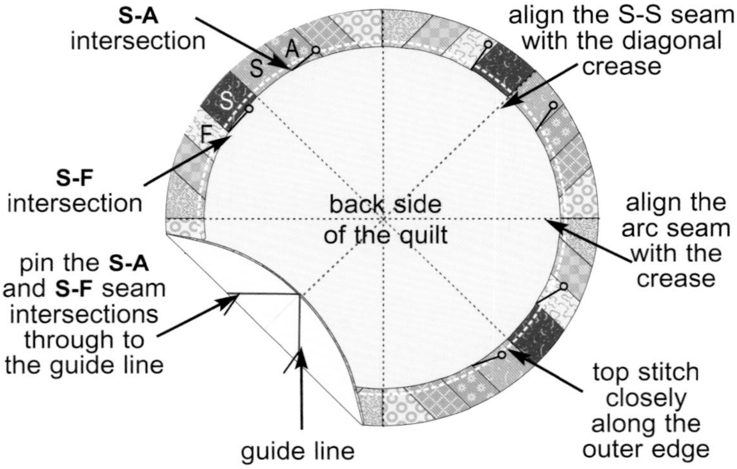
S-A intersection
align the S-S seam with the diagonal crease
S-F intersection
back side of the quilt
align the arc seam with the crease
pin the S-A and S-F seam intersections through to the guide line
top stitch closely along the outer edge
guide line

This is the back of your quilt.

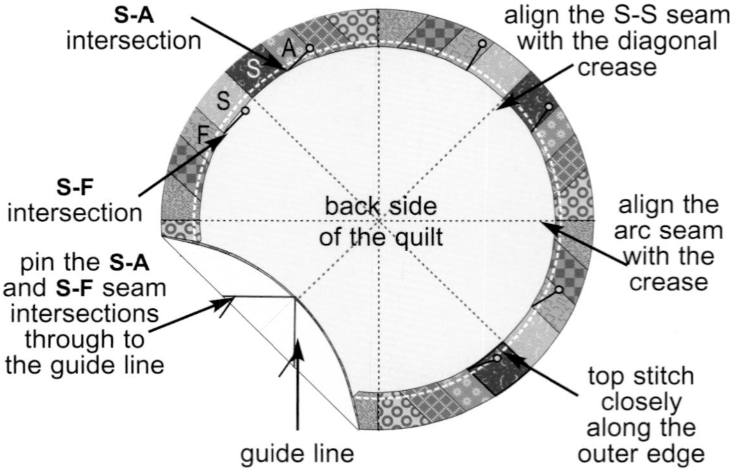
S-A intersection
align the S-S seam with the diagonal crease
S-F intersection
back side of the quilt
align the arc seam with the crease
pin the S-A and S-F seam intersections through to the guide line
top stitch closely along the outer edge
guide line

Quilting

Marking Quilting Design Lines

- Trace a quilting line directly onto the 12 1/2" interior square. Two design options are found on page 54.
- Another option is to trace the design onto tear-away tracing paper, pin the paper to the square, and stitch through the paper.

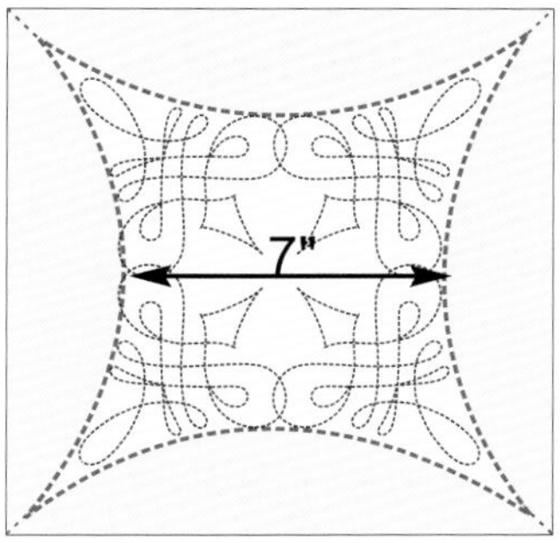
7"

area where interior block fabric is visible

Layering With Basting Spray

- Lightly spray one side of the cotton batting.
- Center the batting square (sprayed side) on the wrong side of the interior square and pat to smooth the layers.
- Lightly spray the back side of the batting.
- Fold the corners and approximate 1/4" edge over the batting square, finger pressing the edge as you go.
- Place the interior square *(with batting)* right side up onto the wrong side of the backing circle.

  The marked guide line will be visible.
- The diagonal creases of the backing and the corner of the interior square should be aligned.
- Pat and smooth the layers together.

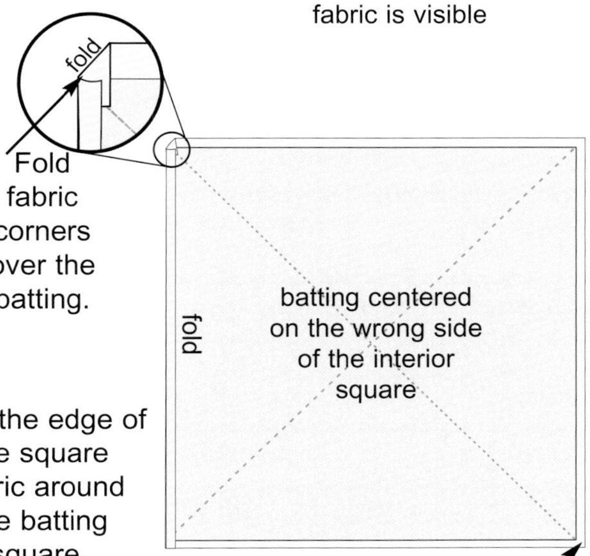
fold
Fold fabric corners over the batting.
fold
batting centered on the wrong side of the interior square
Fold the edge of the square fabric around the batting square.
1/2" of interior fabric extends around the batting

Layering with Hobbs Fusible Batting

- Center the batting on the wrong side of the interior square.
- Fold the corners of the interior square around the batting square and gently press. Use medium heat and just tap the corner down to hold it in place.
- Fold about 1/4" edge over the batting square, pressing the edge as you go.
- Place the interior square *(with batting)* right side up onto the wrong side of the backing circle.

  The marked guide line will be visible.
- The diagonal creases of the backing and the corner of the interior square should be aligned.
- Gently iron the layers together.

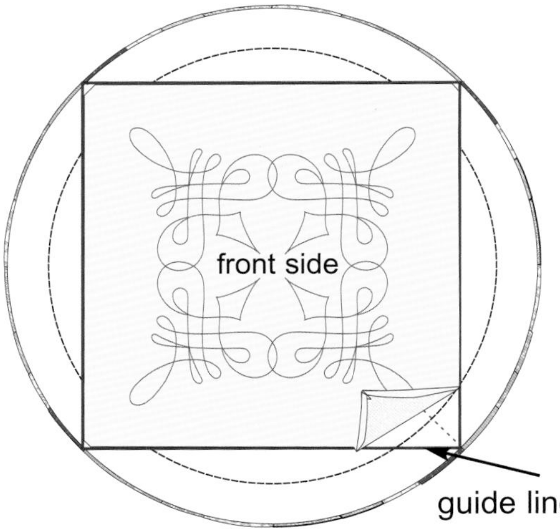
front side
guide line

Place the folded edges in line with the marked guide line, keeping the marked line visible.

Quilting

- Quilt the layers by machine or hand along the lines of the marked quilting design.
- Sometimes the quilting can distort the block out of square. If this happens, gently steam press the layers to eliminate any excess fullness and smooth the circle.

Pieced Scallops

Scallop Definition

Scallops form the curved border of the quilt. Scallops are added to the outer blocks ***before*** the blocks are put together. The corner blocks have two scallops added, the side blocks have one scallop added. The outer edge of each scallop is finished with an arc piece, eliminating the need for traditional binding.

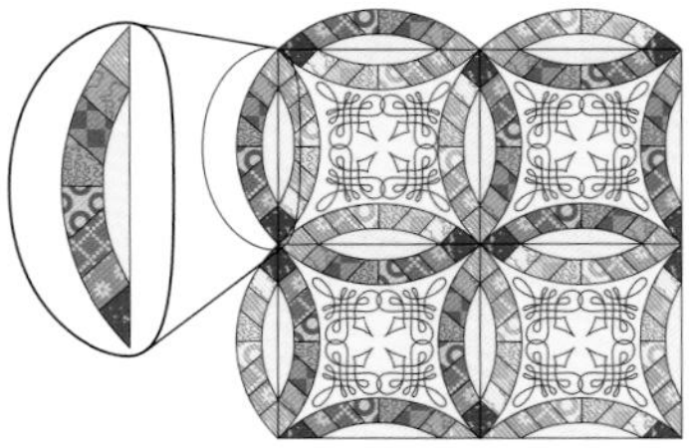

Adding Scallops to Blocks

- Select the blocks which will have scallops added to them. They are the blocks on the outside of the quilt. See page 9 for block placement.
- Unfold the scallop piece.

working from the back

- Place the ***right*** side of the scallop onto the ***back*** side of the block. The corners of the scallop extend 1/4" beyond the backing circle on each side.
- Match the fold line to the marked guide line on the front side of the block.

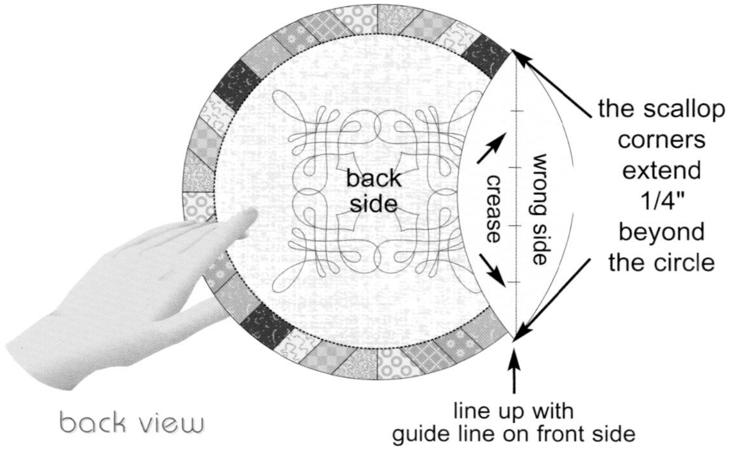
back side
crease
wrong side
the scallop corners extend 1/4" beyond the circle
line up with guide line on front side
back view

Sewing Scallops to Blocks

working from the front

- Pin the scallop to the circle, matching the marked guide line to the crease of the underlying scallop piece.
- Sew precisely along the guide line, back stitching to secure your stitches at the beginning and end of the seam.

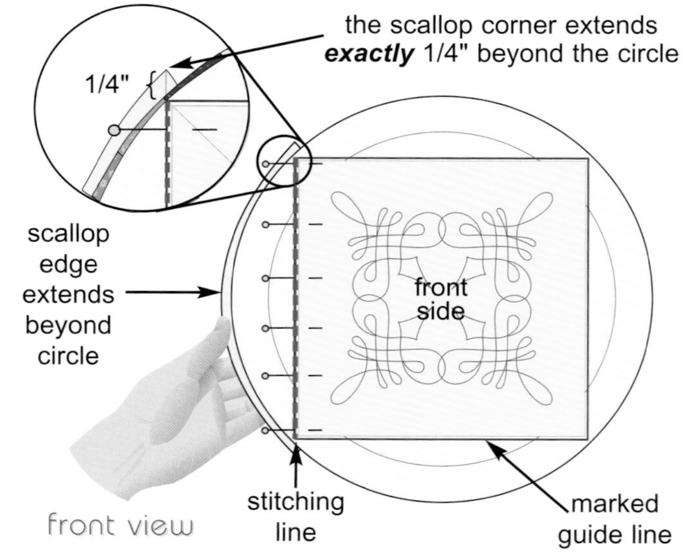
the scallop corner extends ***exactly*** 1/4" beyond the circle
1/4"
scallop edge extends beyond circle
front side
stitching line
marked guide line
front view

When you look at the scallop pages....don't let all the diagrams scare you. Just follow each step, taking note of both the front and back views.

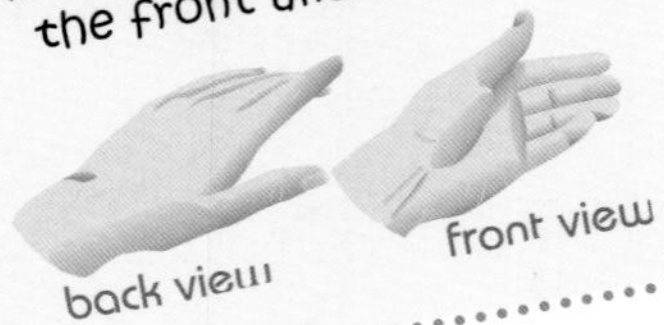
back view
front view

working from the front

- Pin the flap to the interior square to keep it out of your way. Don't catch the scallop piece as you pin.

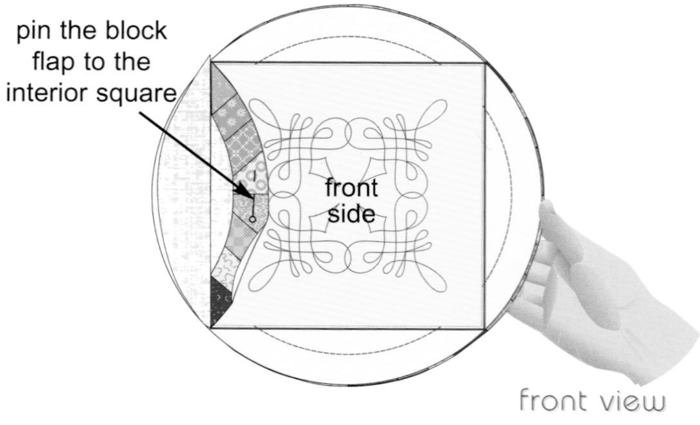
pin the block flap to the interior square
front side
front view

Pieced Scallops

Adding Batting to the Scallop
working from the back
- Center the batting on the scallop even with the stitched line.
- Fold the scallop halves together.
- Pin the edges of the scallop together with the batting between the layers.

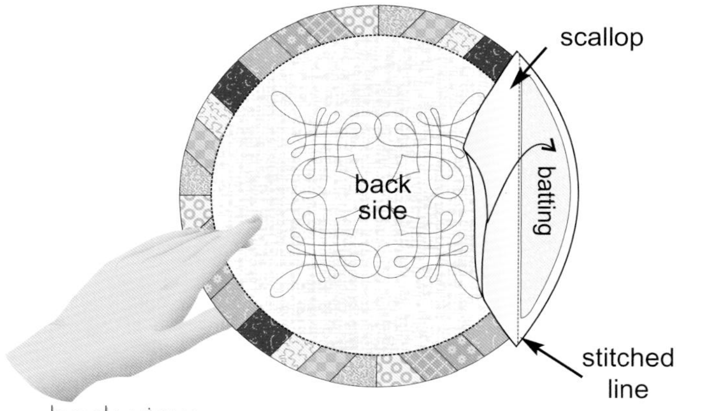

scallop
back side
batting
stitched line

back view

Preparing Arcs for Scallops
- From the arcs you've set aside for scallops, remove the stitching joining the S-S segments of the arc.
- Place the S-F-E-D half on the C-B-A-S half, right sides together.
- Sew the arc halves together joining the D and C segments.
- Turn the inner edge under 1/4" and press.

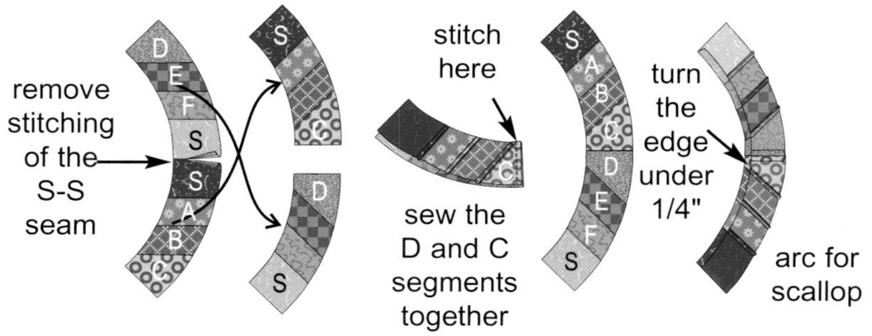

remove stitching of the S-S seam
stitch here
sew the D and C segments together
turn the edge under 1/4"
arc for scallop

Adding an Arc to the Scallop
- Choose an arc of the opposite color family:
  - Set Two arcs to Set One circles.
  - Set One arcs to Set Two circles.
- Spray the arc with spray sizing. While wet, precisely fold under 1/4" along the inner curved edge.
- Press the fold being careful not to stretch the edge.

working from the back
- Pin the ***right*** side of an arc to the back side of the scallop edges, centering it with the scallop.

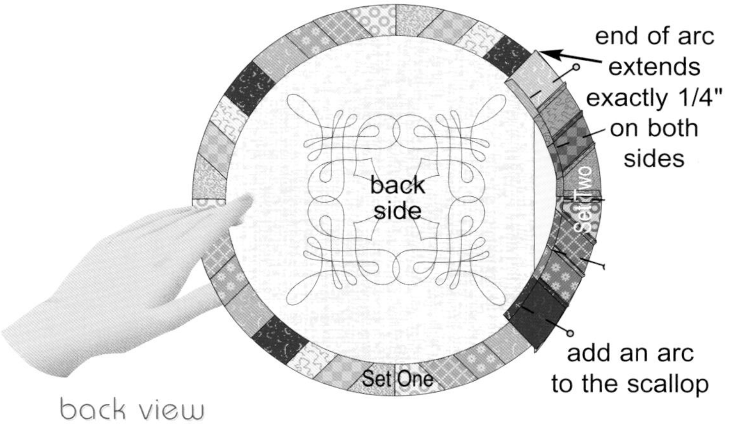

end of arc extends exactly 1/4" on both sides
back side
Set Two
Set One
add an arc to the scallop

back view

working from the front
- Match the end of the arc to the tip of the scallop.
- Stitch from the front side of block, beginning ***precisely*** at the point of intersection, back stitching to secure the stitches at the beginning and end of the seam.

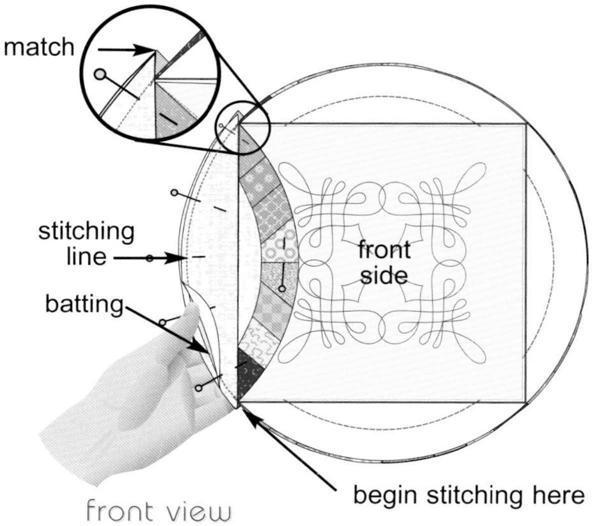

match
stitching line
batting
front side
begin stitching here

front view

Pieced Scallops

working from the back

- Working from the back, fold the corners of the arc even with the seam joining the scallop to the block.
- Finger press this fold line. You may need to adjust this fold slightly when you bring it over to the other side.

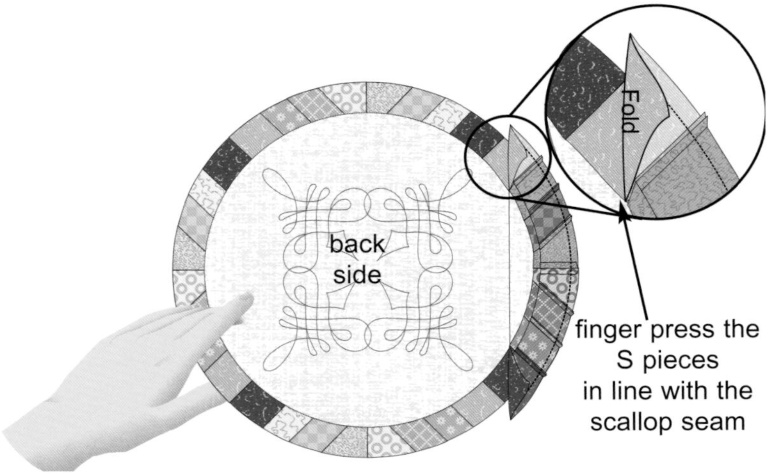
Fold
back
side
finger press the
S pieces
in line with the
scallop seam

back view

working from the front

- Bring the arc over the scallop edge to the front side of the block.
- Wrap the corner of the arc around the seam as shown.
- Using a milliner's needle and matching thread, hide the knot in the seam allowance.
- To reduce the bulk of fabric, fold the scallop "ear", *(that tiny corner of fabric),* to the front and the arc "ear" toward the back.
- Hand sew several stitches to hold the folded "ears".
- Trim fabric ***only*** if necessary.

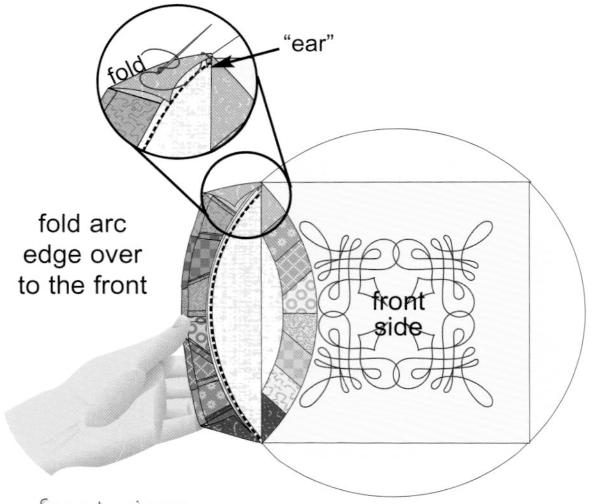
fold
"ear"
fold arc
edge over
to the front
front
side

front view

- Match the S segments and pin, keeping the threaded needle out of the way.
- Hand stitch the folded edge to the matching S segment. Use an invisible stitch to hide your stitches.

- Pin the folded edge of the arc to the scallop.
- Top stitch along the inner edge of the arc.
- Repeat the steps for the remaining scallops.

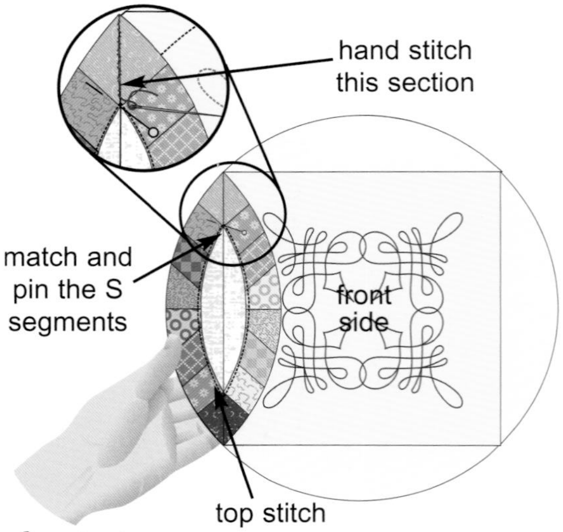
hand stitch
this section
match and
pin the S
segments
front
side
top stitch

front view

Note: Corner blocks will have two scallops added.

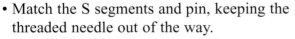

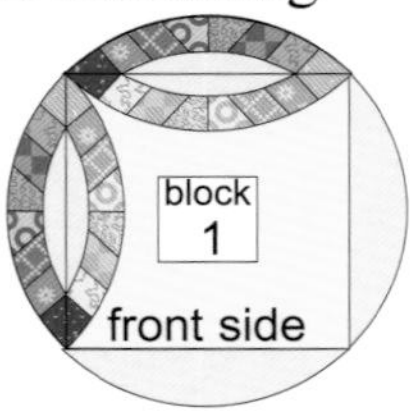
block
1
front side

corner block
label "block 1"

Assembling Pieced Wedding Ring Blocks

A nine block quilt is shown for assembling blocks.

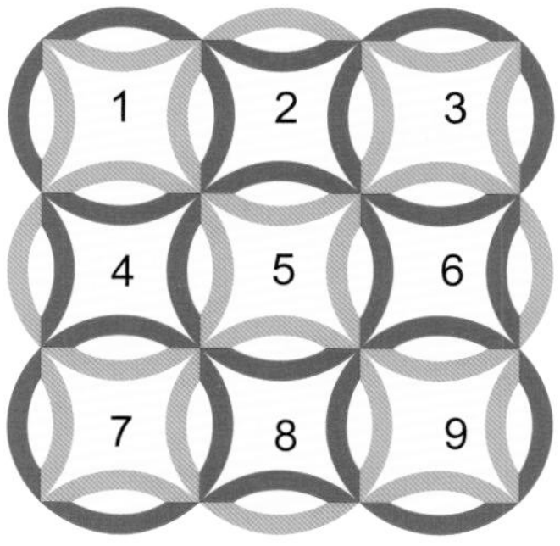
1
2
3
4
5
6
7
8
9

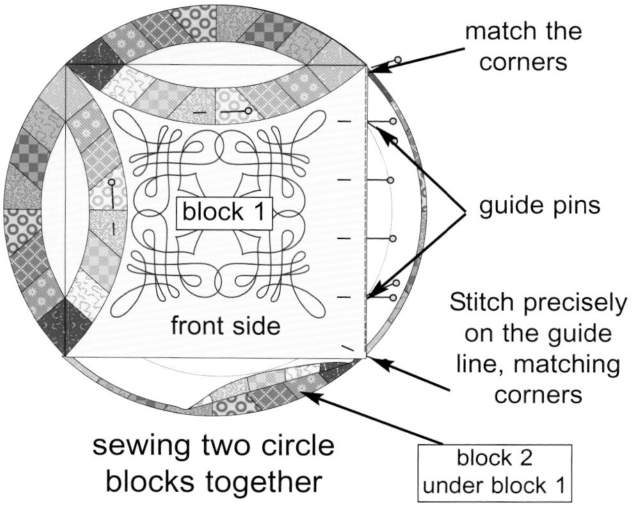
match the corners
guide pins
block 1
front side
Stitch precisely on the guide line, matching corners
block 2 under block 1
sewing two circle blocks together

Sewing the Block Pairs

- Place a Set One block on top of a Set Two block, with the back sides together.
- Match the guide lines of both blocks.
- Place a pin where the S-segment intersects with the guide line.
- Using this pin as a guide, match the corresponding point in the block below.
- Add a second pin to hold this match point securely, leaving the guide pin in its position.
- Repeat for the other point.
- Pin along the guide line, matching it to the guide line of the circle block below. Be sure you pin the edge of the blocks, again matching the guidelines.
- Baste along the marked line and check for accuracy.

Basting will save you time in the long run. Adjustments will be much easier. Just use your longest machine stitching, then just stitch over the top when you know you've got it right.

Before Top stitching...
The best way to beat the bulk is to cinch the corner together using a short stiff hand needle and strong thread. Only put a couple of stitches here--no more than 1/4" into the block. You may also cinch together the ends of the scallops if needed.

- Once you've determined the seam is correct, reset your machine stitching to a shorter stitch length for strength.
- Stitch precisely along the guide line, back stitching to secure your stitches at the beginning and end of the seam.

Top Stitching the Rings

- Pin each flap to each interior square, centering the arc edge with the diagonal fold line of the square. Be sure each flap is nice and smooth before top stitching. Check the back for tucks or wrinkles.
- Top stitch along the outer edge of the arc, securing it to the block.
- Top stitch at each stage of assembly.

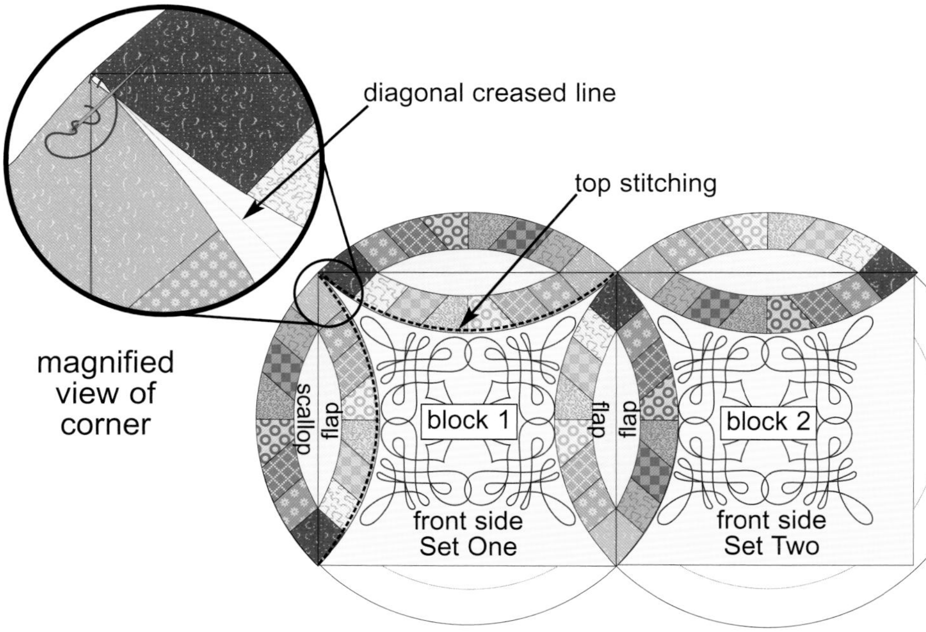
diagonal creased line
top stitching
magnified view of corner
scallop
flap
block 1
flap
flap
block 2
front side Set One
front side Set Two

Assembling Pieced Wedding Ring Blocks

Sewing the Block Foursome

- Place two block pairs together, with back sides together. Notice the rings will be opposite color families.
- Match the guide lines of both blocks.
- Place a pin where each S-segment intersects the guide line.
- Using this pin as a guide, match the corresponding point in the block below.
- Add a second pin to hold the match point securely, leaving the guide pin in its position.

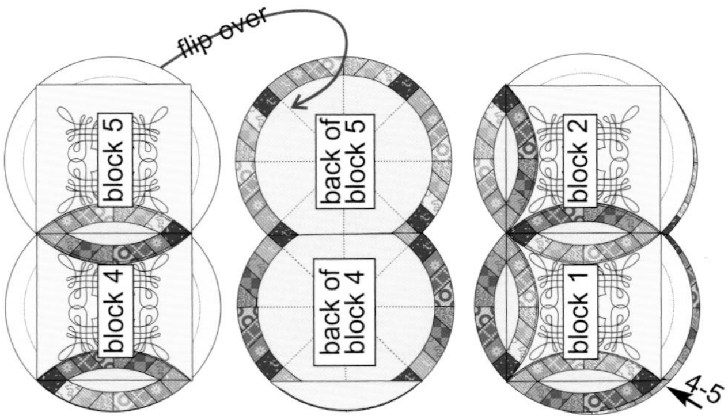
flip over
block 5
block 4
back of block 5
back of block 4
block 2
block 1
4-5

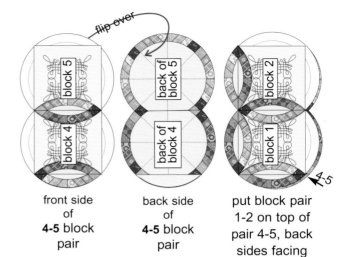

front side of **4-5** block pair

back side of **4-5** block pair

put block pair 1-2 on top of pair 4-5, back sides facing

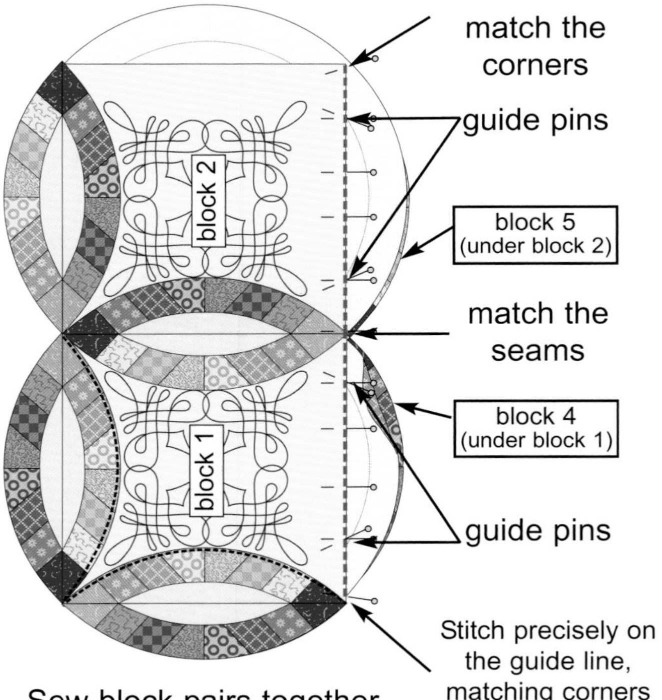
match the corners
guide pins
block 5 (under block 2)
match the seams
block 4 (under block 1)
guide pins
block 2
block 1
Stitch precisely on the guide line, matching corners

Sew block pairs together

- Pin along the guide line, matching it to the guide line of the circle blocks below. Be sure the intersection of each block pair matches as well.
- Stitch precisely along the guide line, back stitching to secure your stitches at the beginning and end of the seam.

- Open the flaps of each block of the **1-2-4-5** foursome.
- Pin the flaps to the interior square, centering the arcs with the diagonal fold line of the square. Be sure both sides of your quilt are nice and smooth before top stitching.

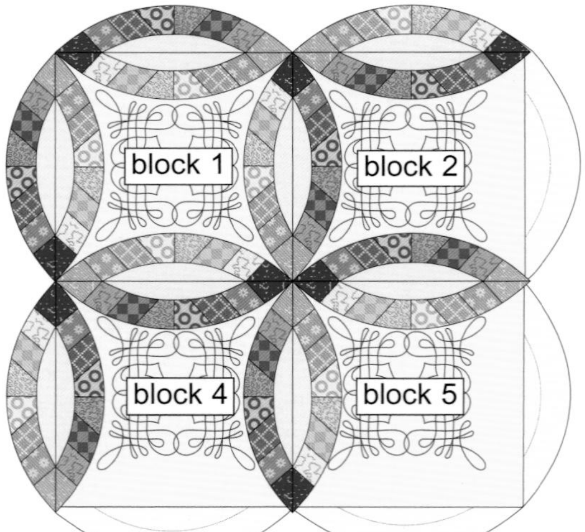
block 1
block 2
block 4
block 5

1-2-4-5 block foursome

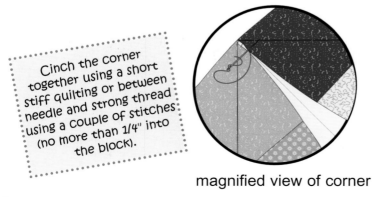

Cinch the corner together using a short stiff quilting or between needle and strong thread using a couple of stitches (no more than 1/4" into the block).

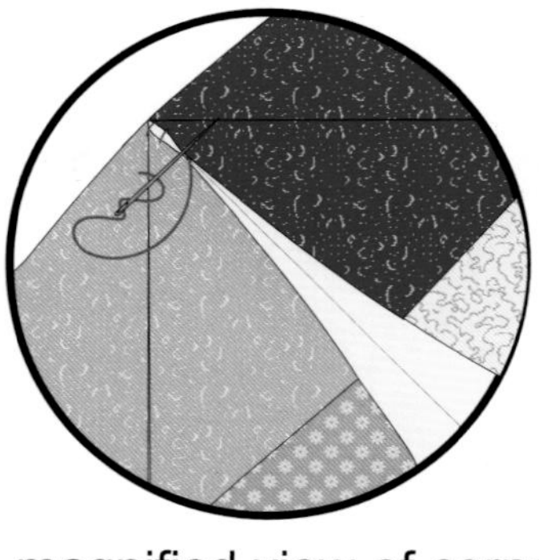

magnified view of corner

- Top stitch along the outer edge of the arc, securing it to the block.
- Top stitch at each stage of assembly.

Assembling Pieced Wedding Ring Blocks

- Sew blocks **3** and **6** together to make a block pair.
- Sew the **1-2-4-5** foursome to the **3-6** block pair.
- Open the flaps of each block and pin to the interior square, centering the arcs with the diagonal fold line. Smooth before top stitching.
- Top stitch along the outer edge of the arc, securing it to the block.
- Alternatives to top stitching include blind stitching with monofilament (clear) thread, decorative stitching with contrasting thread, or adding trim to cover the top stitching.

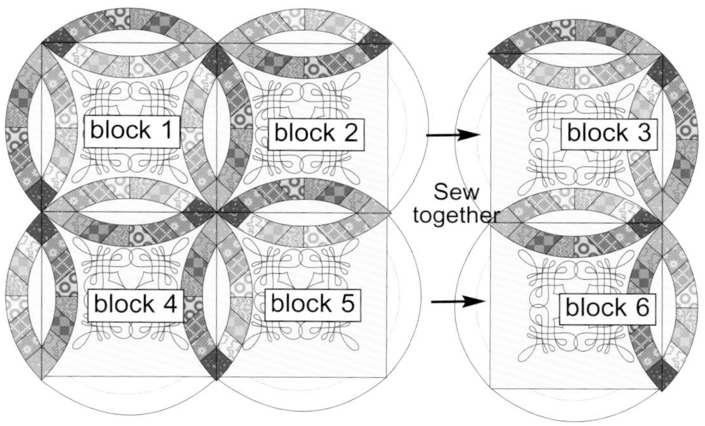
block 1
block 2
block 3
Sew together
block 4
block 5
block 6

1-2-4-5 block foursome

3-6 block pair

- Sew blocks **7** to **8** to make a block pair.
- Sew block **9** to the **7-8** pair.
- Sew the **1-2-3-4-5-6** set to the **7-8-9** set.
- Open the flaps of each block and pin to the interior square, centering each arc with the diagonal fold line. Be sure both sides of your quilt are nice and smooth before top stitching.
- Top stitch along the outer edge of the flap, securing it to the block.

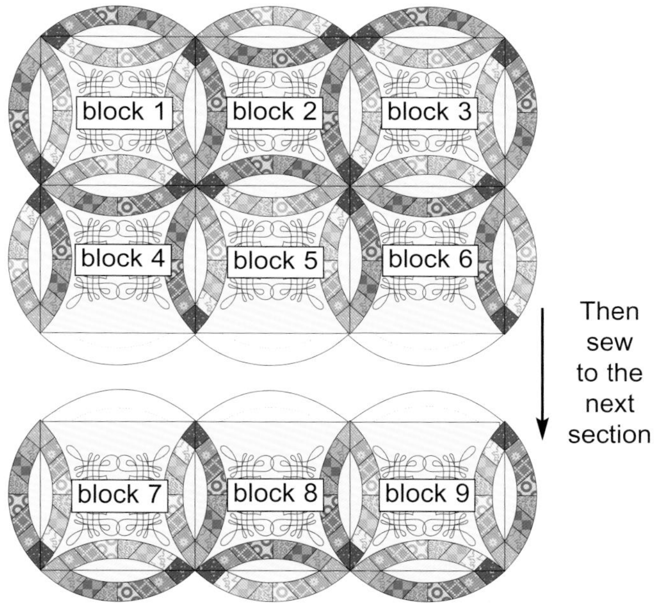
block 1
block 2
block 3
block 4
block 5
block 6
Then sew to the next section
block 7
block 8
block 9

When you've sewn the blocks together...

You're done!

No binding or quilting left to do.

Yeah!

Your wedding ring is now finished.

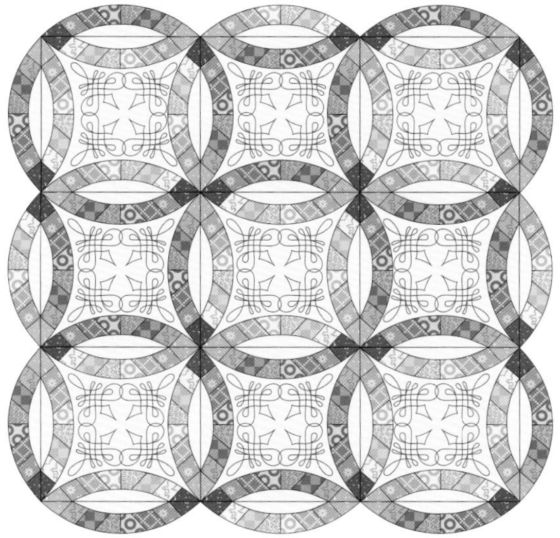

Creative Options for the Interior Squares

There are so many ways to be creative with *Rings That Bind.* The possibilities are endless! Showcase your talents in the center of the wedding ring blocks. Because the blocks are quilted before they are sewn together, you can also apply other techniques at this stage. It's a great place for you to shine and make your quilt uniquely your own.

Victorian Wedding

The interior square is crazy pieced patchwork & embellished with lace medallions, buttons and embroidery.

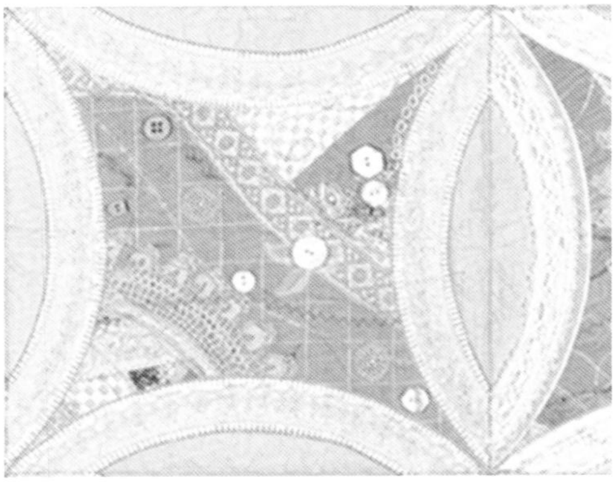

Rose Garden

Appliqued blocks in pink and green give a romantic look to a traditional block.

A 30s Girl

Redwork embroidery with pink top stitching thread doubles as both the embellishment and the quilting.

Creative Options for the Interior Square

Applique:

- hand applique
- mock hand applique
- satin stitch
- buttonhole stitch
- fusible applique
- lace medallions
- reverse applique
- crocheted doilies
- yo-yos
- stained glass applique

Piecing:

- 12" block designs
- paper piecing
- crazy pieced patchwork

Embroidery:

- hand embroidery
- embroidery machine motifs
- free motion embroidery
- bobbin work
- redwork embroidery
- cross stitch
- counted cross stitch
- cut work

Creative Options for the Interior Squares

Photo Transfer:

- wedding photos
- family tree
- vacation memories
- classmates
- fabric scrapbooking

Painting:

- stenciling
- stamping
- crayon
- calligraphy
- dyeing
- flower pounding

Trapunto:

- stuffed from behind method
- cut-away batting method
- corded Italian trapunto

Embellishment:

- beading
- buttons
- lace
- silk flowers stitched on
- pins
- sport ribbons

Creative Fabric Choices:

- novelty prints
- large floral prints
- elegant satins and silks
- heirloom handkerchiefs
- batiks
- tie dyes

Wedding photo printed on fabric and embellished with lace (wallhanging made with the 15" Arc-Ease tool, ring bearer's pillow made with the 9" tool - see page 56 for ordering information)

Spring

Hand painted lilacs with stippled petals brighten the soft green fabric. Thread sketched leaves tumble over the arcs and onto the interior squares.

Broderie Perse In Blues

Most of the arcs were made from a floral fabric. Flowers cut from this fabric were also free form appliqued in the centers of some blocks and embellished with black thread sketching.

Creative Options for the Rings

The interlocking rings inspire creativity. Top stitching attaches the arcs to both the backing circle and the block itself. This gives the rings added dimension. In addition to being functional, this stitching can be decorative, adding charm and interest to your wedding ring quilt.

Victorian Wedding

The rings are decorated with flat lace and edged with a blanket stitch in gold metallic thread.

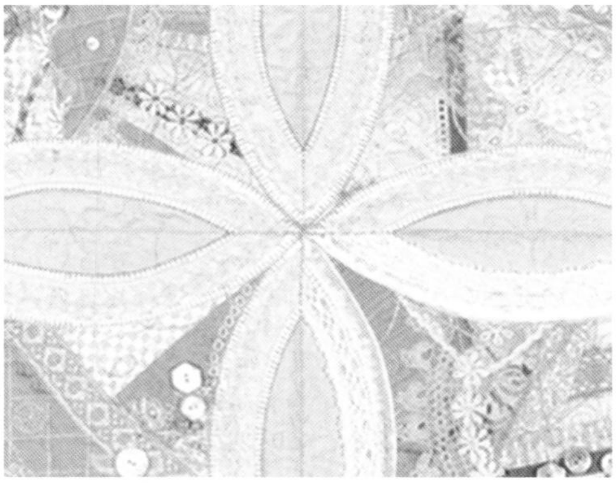

Lake House Trellis

Rings are trimmed with rick rack, piping, and lace.
The arcs are made from a coordinating striped fabric.

Elegance in Trapunto

Arcs were cut from strip sets stitched with lace and trim along seam lines.

Top Stitching the Edges:

- decorative stitches on your machine
- hand finishes such as a blanket stitch
- invisible thread with a blind hem stitch
- decorative threads:
  - metallic or rayon, fine or heavy

Decorating the Rings:

- flat lace on seamless arcs
- painting the arcs
- stenciled designs
- embroidered names
- couched trims

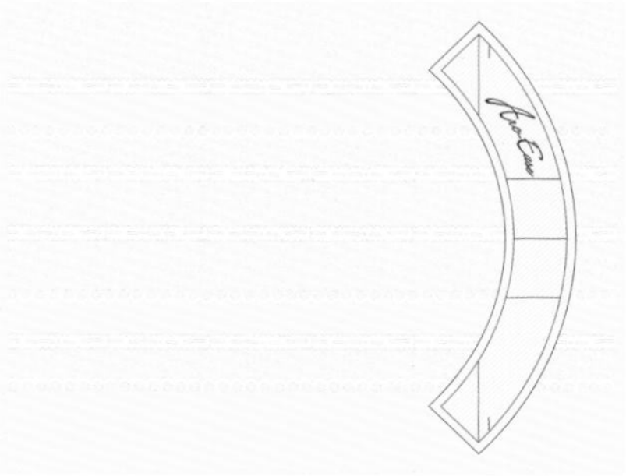

Embellishing the Strip Sets:

- arcs from strip sets with lace,
  decorative stitching, and trim along seam lines
- crazy pieced patchwork
- string pieced sets

Fabric Choices:

- stripes
- floral prints
- multiple fabrics
- elegant fabrics

Trimming the Ring Edges:

- rick rack
- lace
- cording
- piping
- folded flat piping
- braid

Creative Options for the Rings

Tips for adding rick rack

Inner Edge

- Sew the rick rack (or other trim) to the **right** side of the inner ring along the raw edge, ***before*** pressing the edge under.
- Overlap the rick rack at the arc seam.
- Turn the edge under using the stitching as a guide and press. The rick rack will help roll the edge.
- Repeat the process for the inner curve of the scallops.

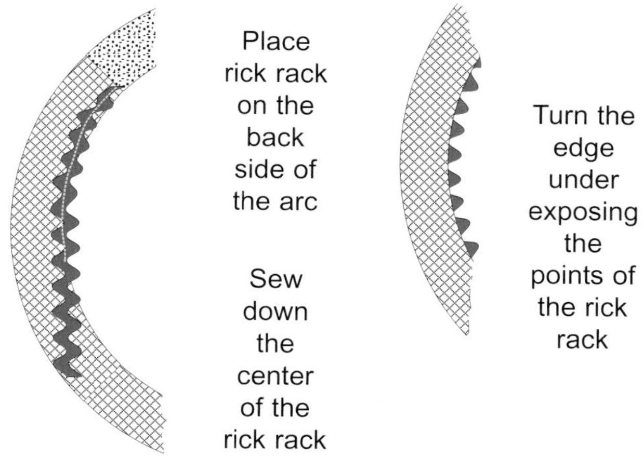
Place rick rack on the back side of the arc
Sew down the center of the rick rack
Turn the edge under exposing the points of the rick rack

Outer Edge

- Add rick rack to the outer edge of the ring ***after*** the blocks are assembled.
- Measure about 9 1/4" sections of rick rack.
- As you top stitch the flaps down, place the rick rack between the flap and the square. Catch the rick rack as you top stitch the edges.
- The ends of the rick rack section are poked under the flap, leaving no rick rack added to the corner area.
- For the outer edge of the scallop, trim can be sewn in the seam adding the arc to the scallop edge, or from the back of the quilt.

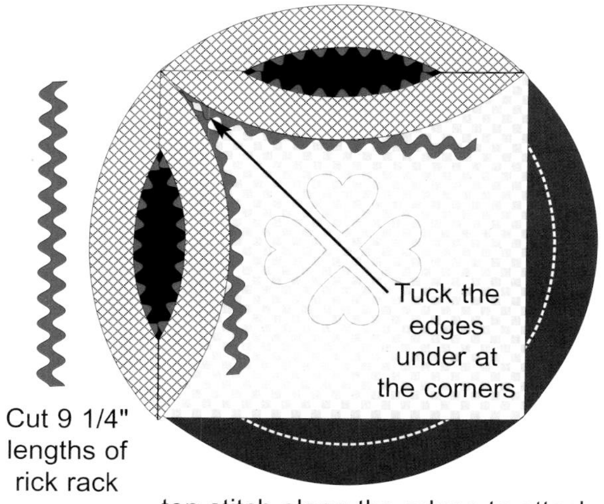
Tuck the edges under at the corners
Cut 9 1/4" lengths of rick rack
top stitch along the edges to attach both the flap and the rick rack

Flat Piping

Bias flat folded piping is another option for trimming the arc edges. The *Lake House Trellis* quilt is edged with black lace, rick rack and flat piping.

To make your piping:

- Cut a 6 1/2" strip of piping fabric.
- Cut the strip at a 45 degree angle. Discard the triangle.
- Cut 1" wide bias strips.
- Fold the strips in half lengthwise and insert as you would other trims.

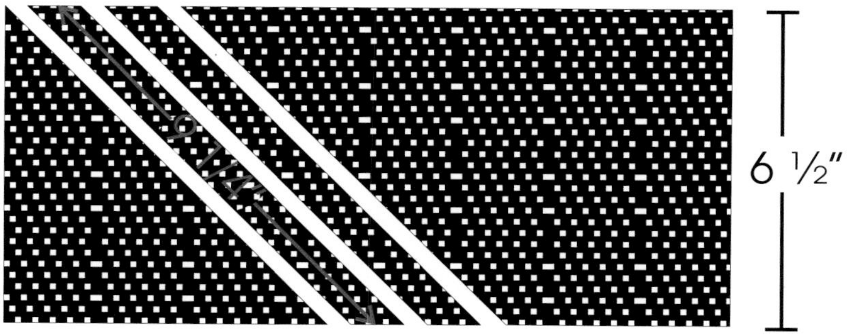
6 ½"

Trim (rick rack, lace, braid, etc.)	Single 1	Runner 1 x 3	Wall 2 x 2	Baby 3 x 3	Lap 5 x 5	Twin 5 x 7	Double 6 x 7	Queen 7 x 8	King 8 x 8
Sewn on one side of the arcs	3 1/4 yd	7 5/8 yd	9 1/4 yd	18 1/4 yd	45 yd	62 yd	73 yd	95 yd	108 yd
Sewn on both sides of the arcs	5 3/4 yd	13 3/4 yd	16 1/2 yd	33 1/2 yd	81 1/2 yd	111 yd	132 yd	173 yd	196 yd

Creative Options for Working with Stripes

- Stripes create visual movement and a secondary pattern. Striped fabric offers many possibilities. Stripes used for rings create a secondary pattern, both on the front and the back of the quilt. Stripes used for the backing circles also create secondary patterns in the football area and the backing. The fall wallhanging shows this application

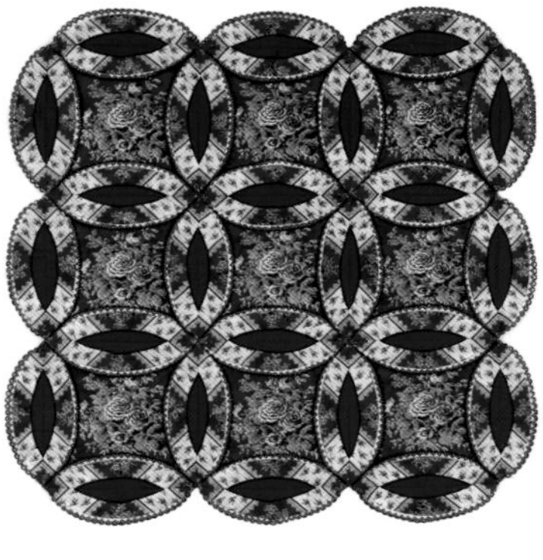

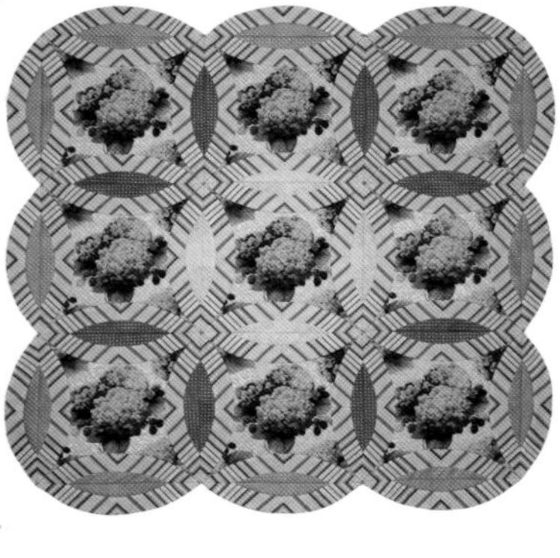

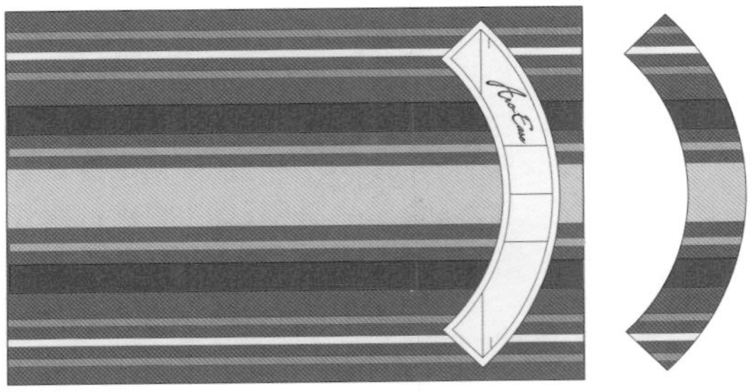

- When selecting striped fabric for the arcs, the scale and repeat of the stripe needs to be considered. Symmetrical stripes are necessary. Stripes that repeat every 1 1/2" to 2 1/2" may give the illusion of a pieced arc.

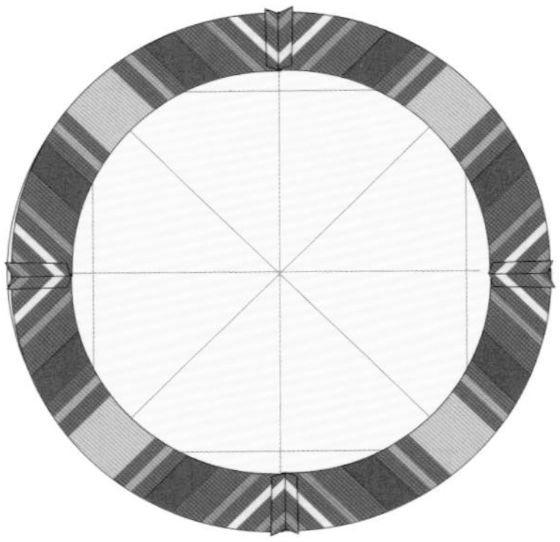

- Rotate the ring so the seam joining the arcs matches the center horizontal and vertical crease lines.

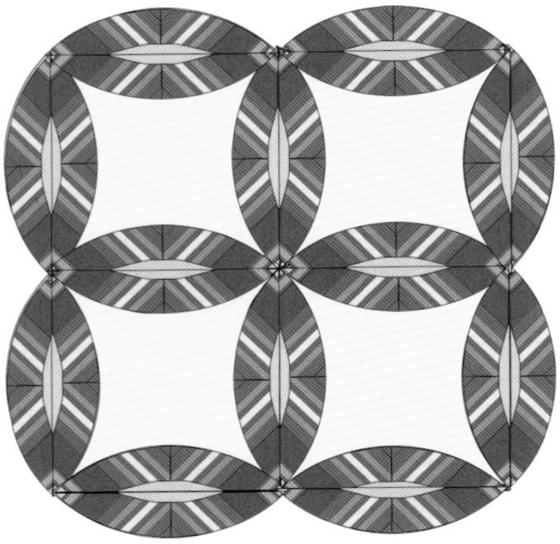

Where did the pink stripe go? It's now on the back side of the quilt!

Calculating Yardage

If you want to make your quilt a size we haven't included in the yardage charts, here are some helpful formulas:

The number of blocks equals the number of backing circles plus interior squares.

 # scallops = (# across x 2) + (# down x 2)

The number of scallops equals the number of blocks across times two plus the number of blocks down times two.

 # arcs = (# blocks x 4) + (# scallops)

The number of arcs equals the number of blocks times four plus the number of scallops.

Yardage for the backing equals the number of blocks divided by two (rounded up) times 18 plus the number of scallops divided by 3 times 6.

$$\text{backing yardage} = \left(\frac{\#\ \text{blocks}^*}{2} \times 18\right) + \left(\frac{\#\ \text{scallops}}{3} \times 6\right)$$

Yardage for each pieced backing fabric (if each backing square uses four colors) equals the number of blocks divided by four, (rounded up) times 9.5.

$$\underset{\text{(four colors)}}{\text{pieced back yardage}} = \frac{\#\ \text{blocks}^*}{4} \times 9.5$$

Yardage for the interior squares equals the number of blocks divided by three times 12.5.

$$\text{interior square yardage} = \frac{\#\ \text{blocks}^*}{3} \times 12.5$$

Yardage for the arcs equals the number of arcs divided by twelve times 13.

 # arcs = (# blocks x 4) + (# scallops)

*rounded to the nearest whole number

Creative Options for Pieced Backing

When the football areas are different colors within the same block, you add a secondary design element. Examples are the *Salsa* quilt and the *Imperial Wedding* quilt. Piecing the backing circles is the secret to this design option. As an added bonus, the back of the quilt is a wonderful surprise.

Designing

Plan your pieced backed *Rings That Bind* quilt by copying and coloring the grid found on page 53. Assign each block a number. Now you're ready to translate your design to the pieced backing.

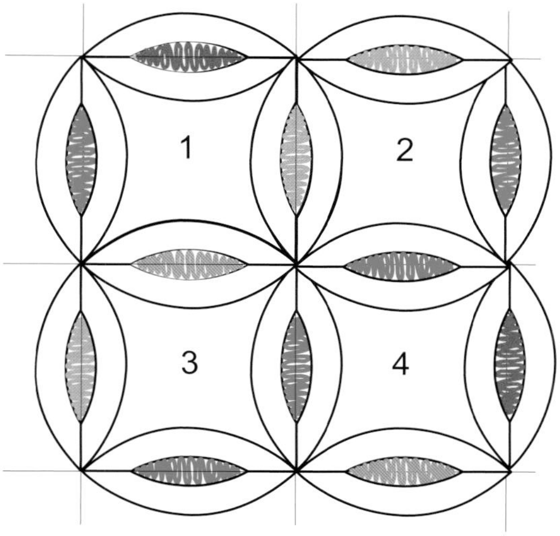
1
2
3
4

color the design grid

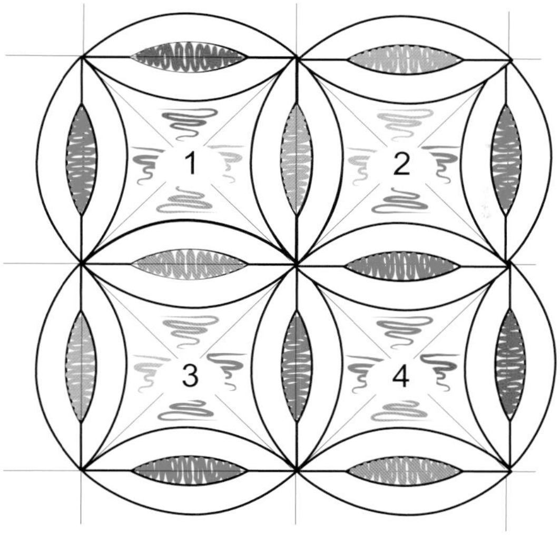
1
2
3
4

add diagonal lines and color in corresponding backing areas

Making the Pieced Backing

- Approach each block individually.
- For each block, cut ***four*** 9 1/2" squares of backing fabric.
- Place squares of backing on point, ***wrong*** side up, to match your colored design.
- Sew the four 9 1/2" squares together to make one 18 1/2" pieced backing square.
- Press the seam allowances open, as you go.

Cutting the Scallop Pieces

- For each scallop, cut a 6" x 13" strip of fabric of the color matching the coordinating block.
- Fold the rectangle in half lengthwise and press a crease.
- Place the Arc-Ease tool on the crease and cut each scallop piece.
- For the example shown, cut three blue, two green, two rose and one orange scallop.

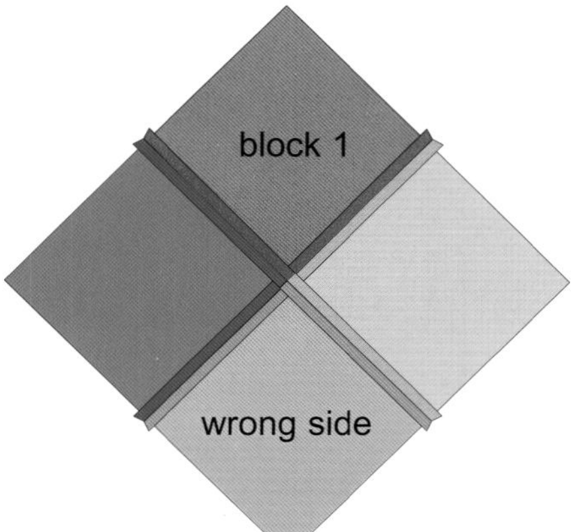
block 1
wrong side

piece the backing square

cut the scallops using the Arc-Ease tool

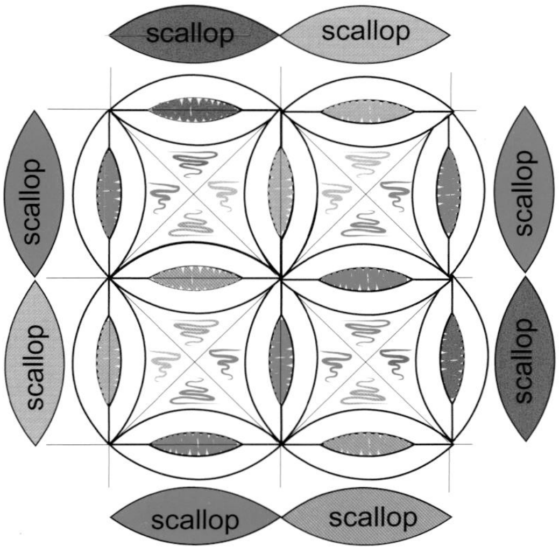
scallop
scallop
scallop
scallop
scallop
scallop
scallop
scallop

- Place a square ruler on the right side of the pieced backing, with the 8 3/4" measurement aligned to the seams.
- Cut little notches or mark carefully to establish both 8 3/4" points.
- Rotate the square and repeat this step.

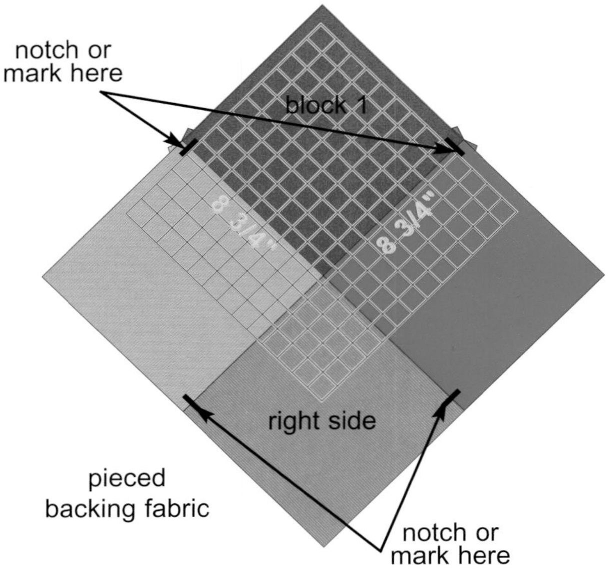
notch or
mark here
block 1
8 3/4"
8 3/4"
right side
pieced
backing fabric
notch or
mark here

- Place the Arc-Ease tool onto one quadrant of the backing square, carefully aligning the tool to both 8 3/4" notches.
- Cut along the outside of the arc in each quadrant, cutting out the circle.
- Label each backing circle with its assigned number noting the portion which is the top of the quilt. The numbering keeps the blocks in order when sewing them together.

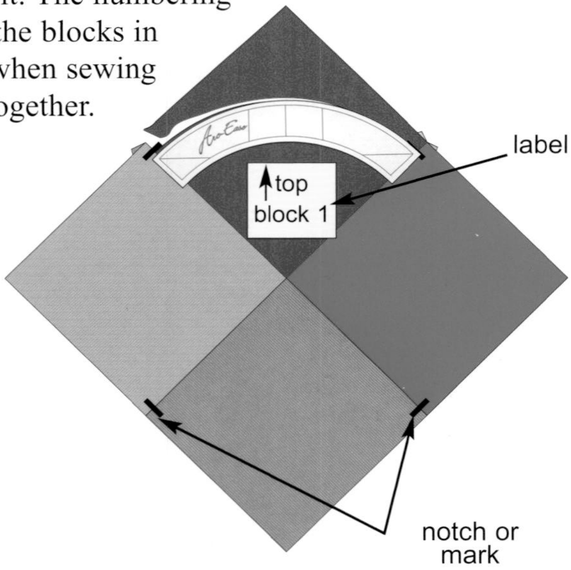
label
top
block 1
notch or
mark

- Measure the circle to be sure the diameter is exactly 17 1/2".
- Fold the circle diagonally to establish precise 1/8 sections.
- Press the folds into creases. The creases will be used later for placement.
- Mark the 12" guide line onto the backing circle, aligning corners of the guide line to the seams.

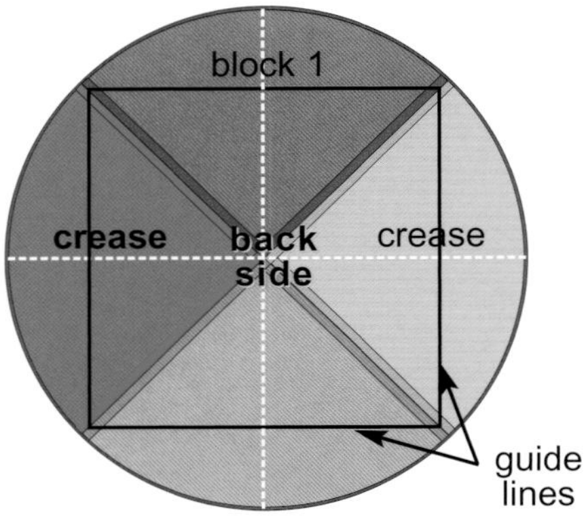
block 1
crease
back
side
crease
guide
lines

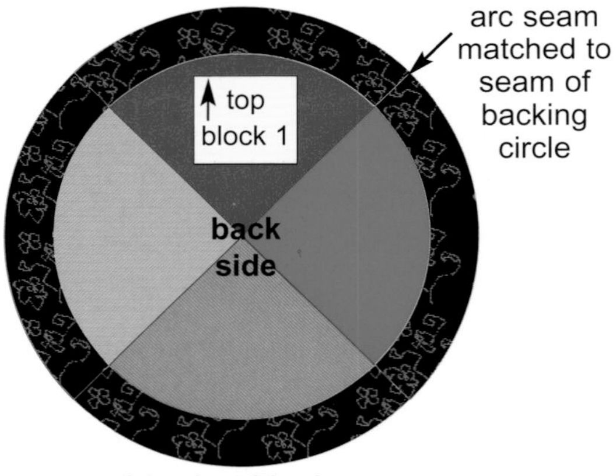
arc seam
matched to
seam of
backing
circle
top
block 1
back
side

block with ring

Completing a Pieced Back Quilt

- Go to page 37 to complete your project.
- Follow the design grid numbers when assembling the blocks.
- When placing blocks together, check to see that the backgrounds match before sewing.

Design Grid

Use the design grid for planning your fabric placement.

The design grid may be photocopied for your personal designing needs.

Quilting Designs

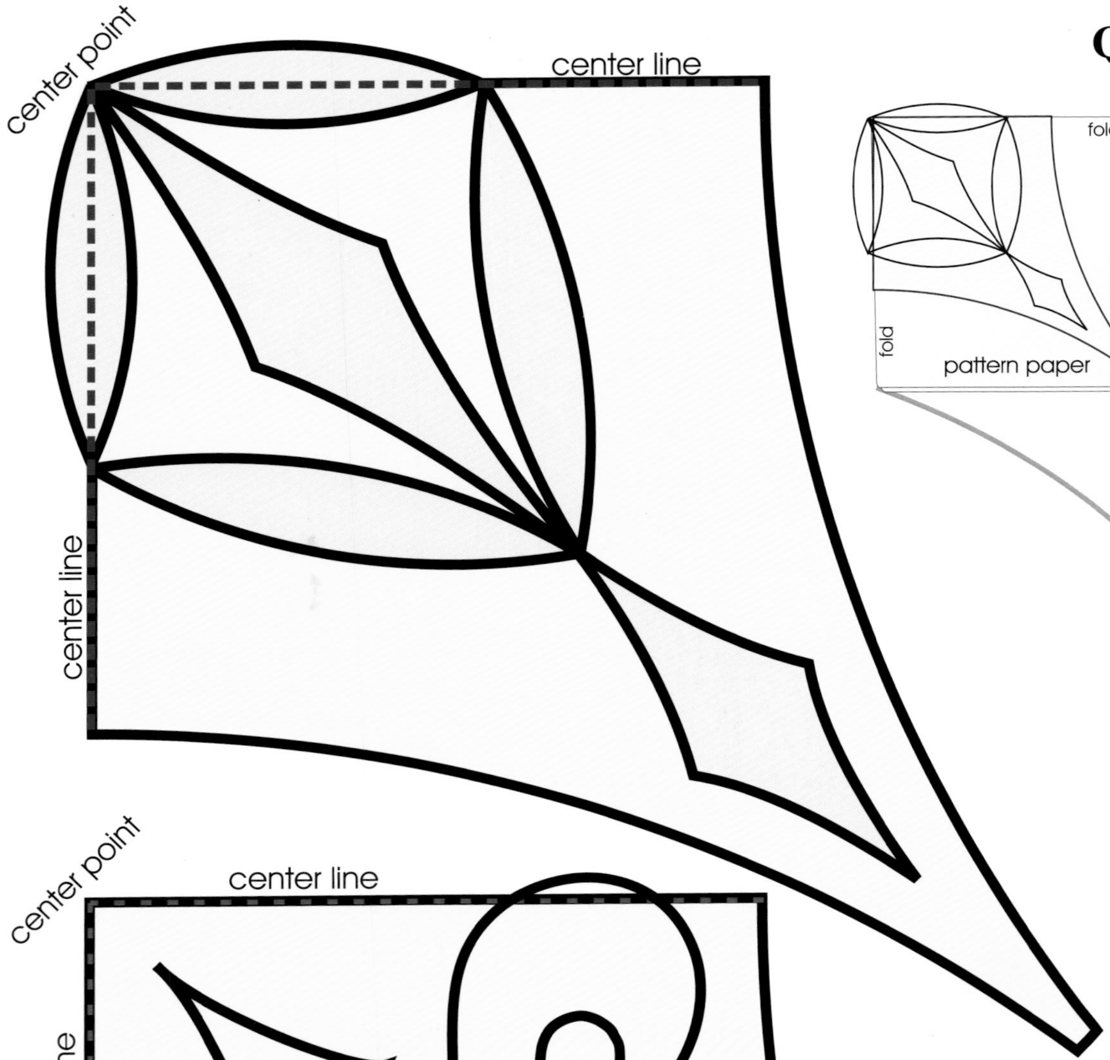

center point
center line
center line

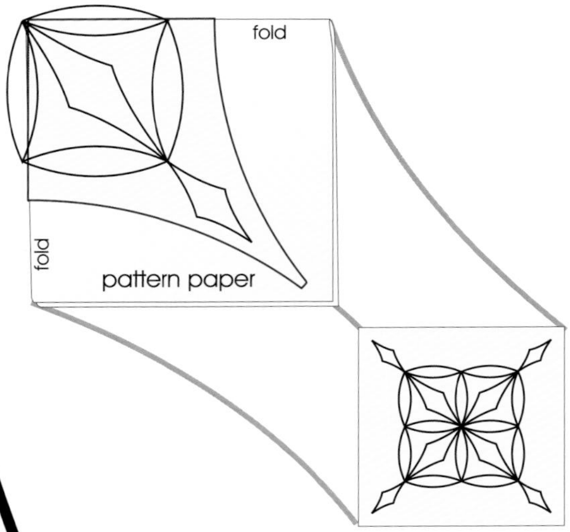

fold
fold
pattern paper

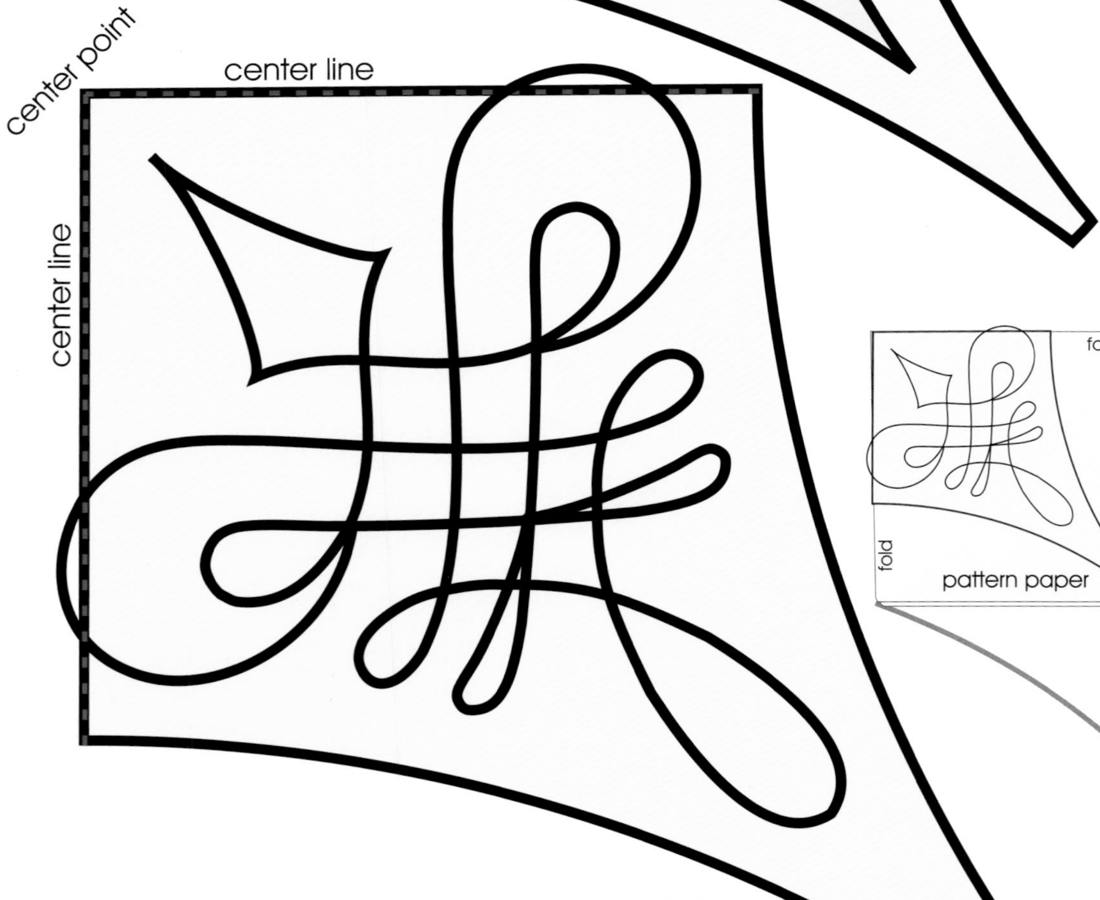

center point
center line
center line

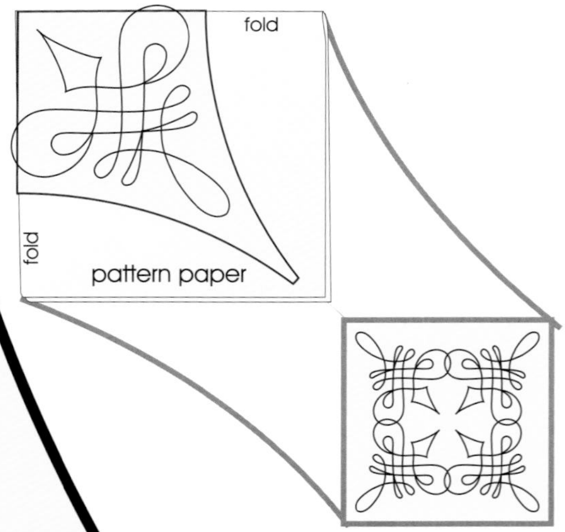

fold
fold
pattern paper

Marking Quilting Design Lines

- Trace the design onto tearaway tracing paper, pin the paper to the square, and stitch through the paper.
- Another option is to trace the design directly onto the fabric using a fabric safe pencil.

Both quilting designs are available as stencils from Phillips Fiber Art.
See page 56 to order.

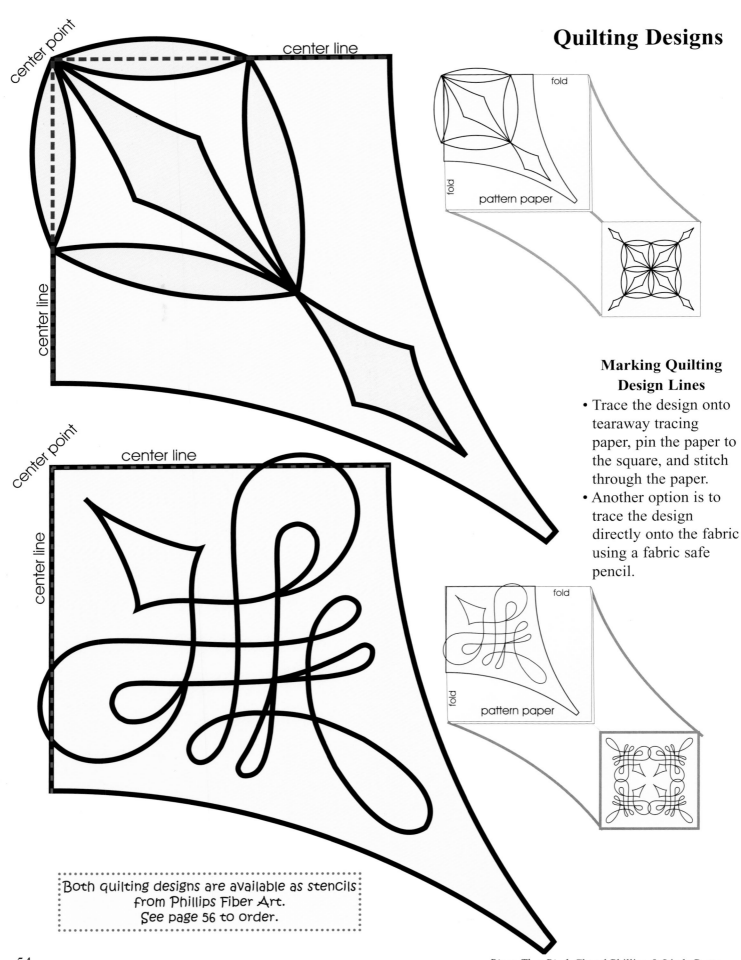

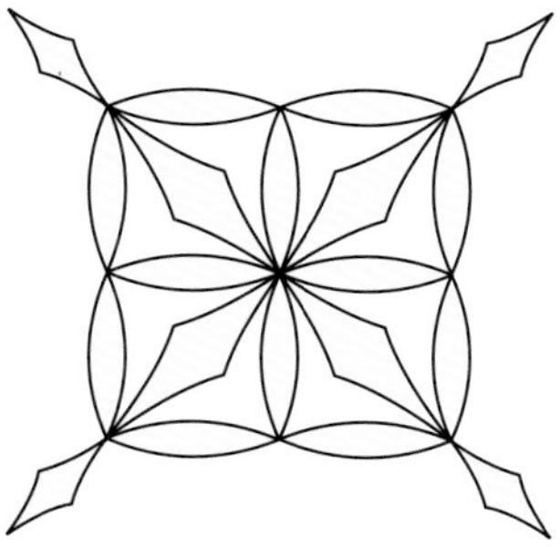

The quilting design shown here lends itself to trapunto. You can see an example of the quilt on the back cover.

Trapunto

Here's a brief explanation of the technique:

- Layer your interior square with an 11 1/2" square of fluffy polyester batting and no backing.
- Stitch around the quilting design.
- Turn the block over and cut away the batting, leaving batting in the areas you want to puff out.
- Layer the block with cotton batting and your backing circle.
- Restitch the quilting lines.
- Closely stipple the background areas, remembering what you quilt, flattens, and what you don't quilt, puffs out.

Applique Pattern

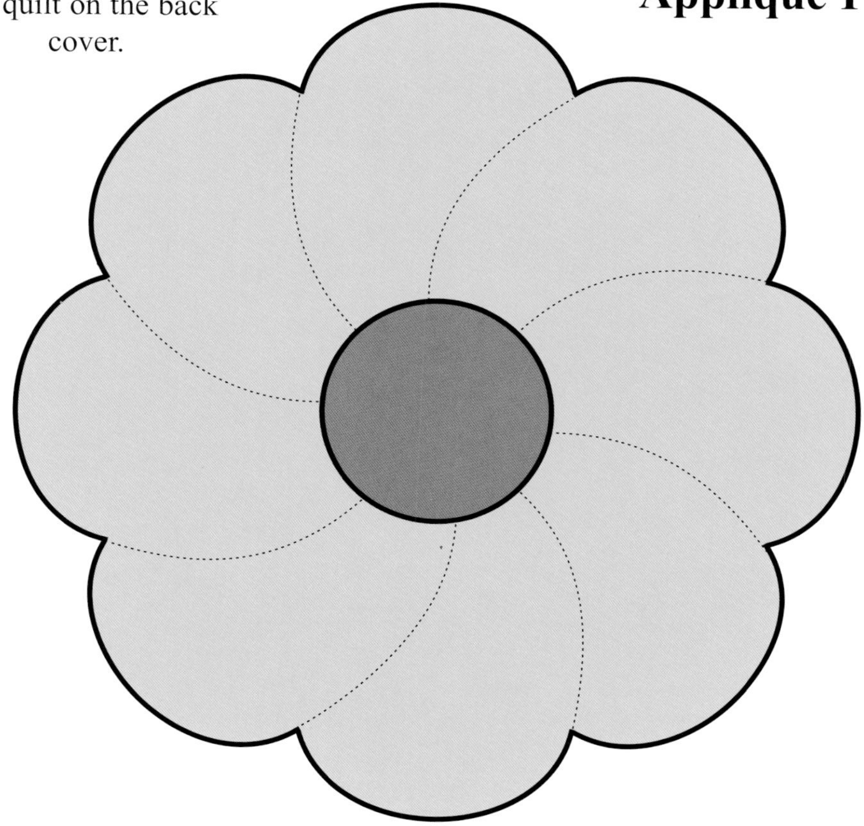

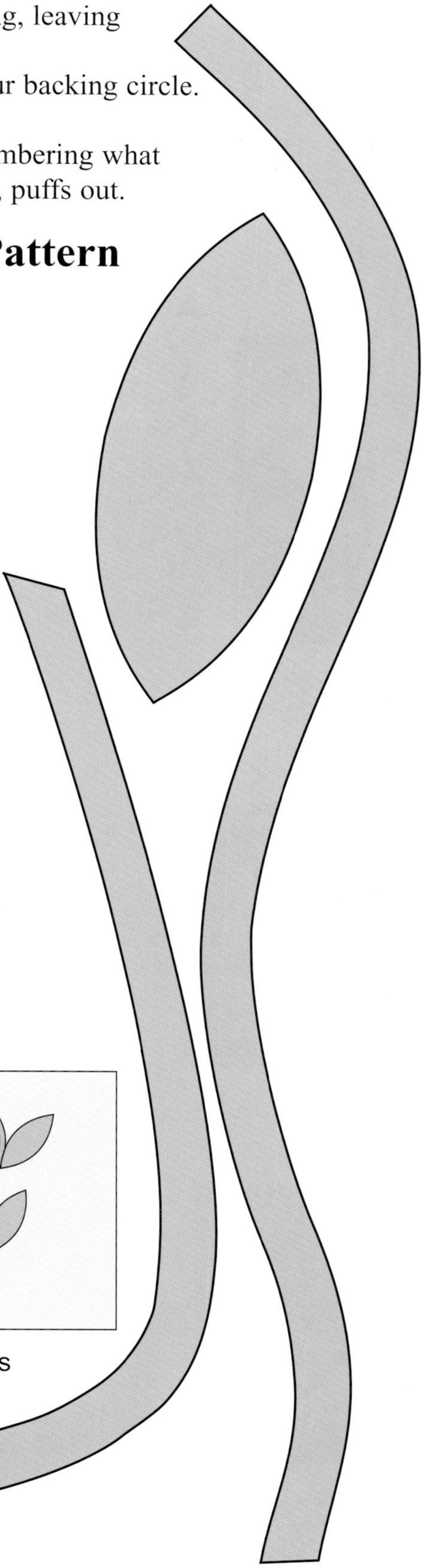

suggested placement for flowers, stems, and leaves

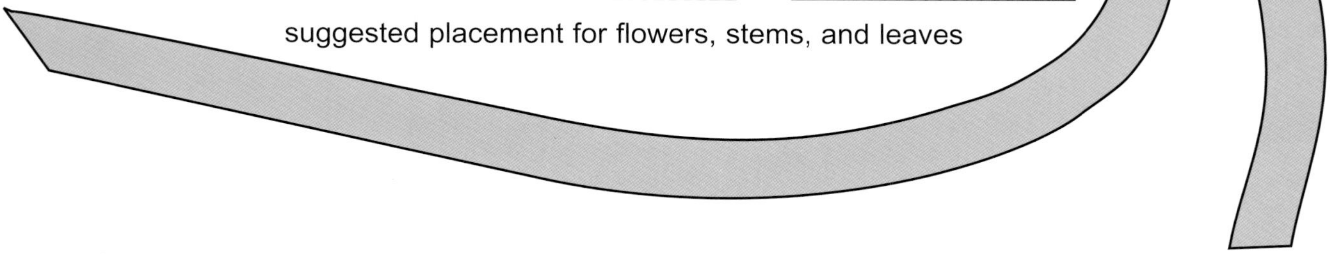

Phillips Fiber Art Products

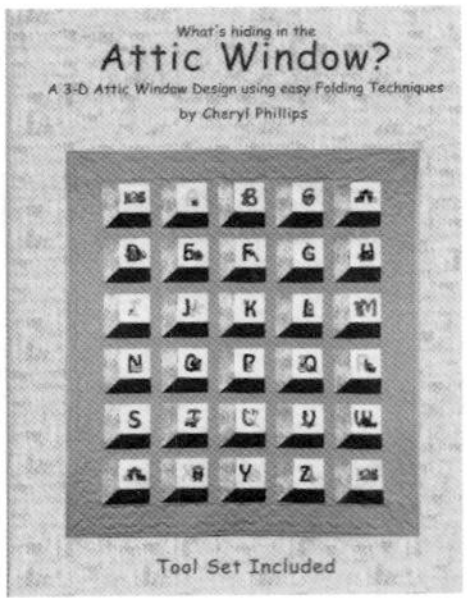
What's hiding in the
Attic Window?
Tool Set Included
What's Hiding in the Attic Window?
with set of 2 or 6 tools

Arc-Ease Tools

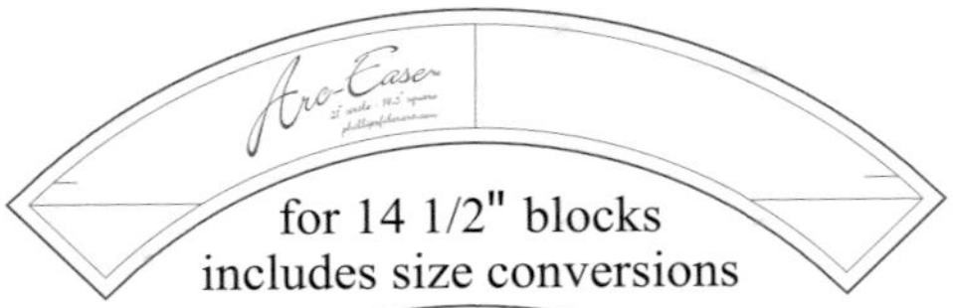
for 14 1/2" blocks
includes size conversions

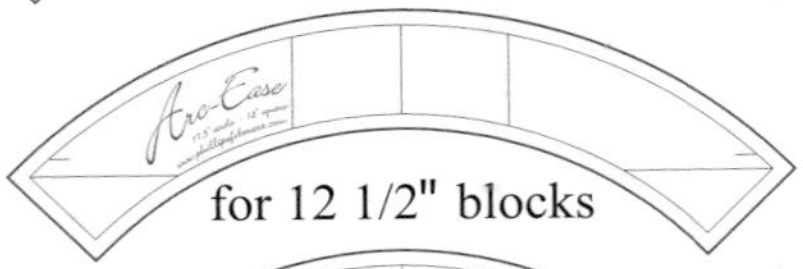
for 12 1/2" blocks

for 9" blocks
includes size conversions

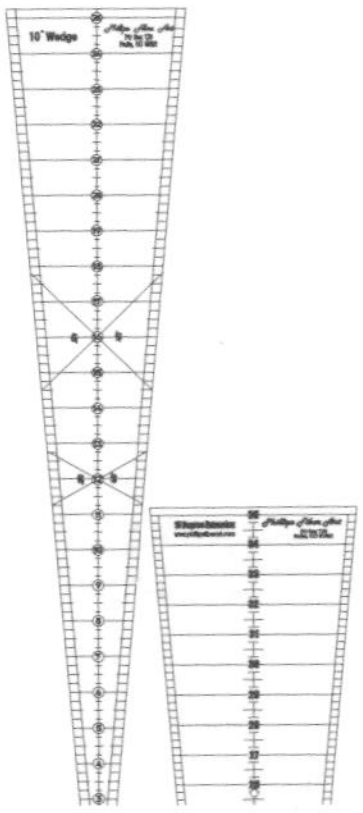
10 Degree Wedge
& 10 Degree Wedge
Extension

Quilts Without Corners
By Cheryl Phillips
Quilts Without
Corners

Bargello
Color Wheel
Color Wheel Bargello
includes wedge tool

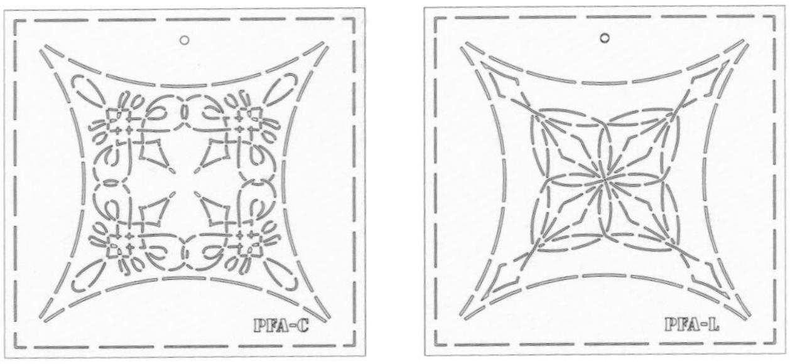
PFA-C
PFA-L
Rings That Bind multi-use stencils
each design includes 12" guide line,
viewing area, and quilting design

WedgeWorks II
Cheryl Phillips
Wedgeworks II
the 3-D Mariner's
Compass
includes two tools

Cheryl Phillips
Circle A Round
Making Circles
FUN!
Circle A Round

Phillips Fiber Art
PO Box 173
Fruita, CO 81521
1-800-982-8166 (orders)
970-858-1698

info@phillipsfiberart.com or
www.phillipsfiberart.com

Wedge Tool Included
WedgeWorks
Wedgeworks
includes 15 degree
wedge tool

FOLK STARS
Fast & Fun—because they're FOLDED!
Fold a square – Make a star!
Folk Star Quilts
includes tool

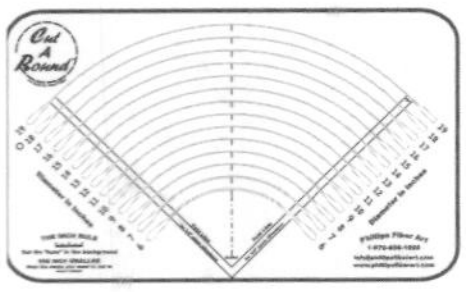
Standard 6" to 19"

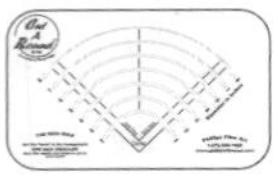
Mini 2" to 6"

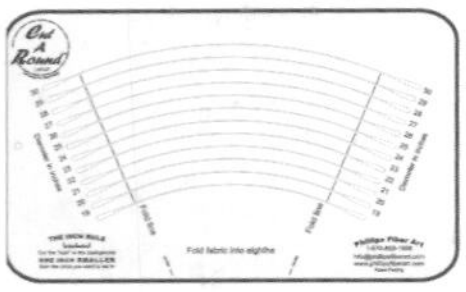
Large 19" to 30"

Cut A Round
Cut perfect circles
3 tool sizes

For class information contact
Cheryl through Phillips Fiber Art
(address above)
or contact:
Linda Pysto
3138 Sisk
Las Vegas, NV 89108
702-645-7820

Granny Lu's
Flower
Garden
Granny Lu's Flower
Garden
includes tool and stencil